Stefan Buczacki

Best Ground Cover

hamlyn

Creative Director Keith Martin
Executive Editor Julian Brown
Design Manager Bryan Dunn
Designer Tony Truscott
Editorial Manager Jane Birch
Production Controller Sarah Scanlon
Picture Researcher Charlotte Deane

First published in Great Britain in 2000
by Hamlyn
an imprint of Octopus Publishing Limited
2–4 Heron Quays, London, E14 4JP

Distributed in the United States by
Sterling Publishing Co, Inc., 387 Park Avenue South,
New York, NY 10016-8810

© Octopus Publishing Group Limited 2000
Text © Stefan Buczacki 2000
Design © Octopus Publishing Group Limited 2000

ISBN 0 600 60040 8

All rights reserved. No part of this publication may
be reproduced, stored in a retrieval system, or
transmitted in any form or by any means, mechanical,
photocopying, recording or otherwise, without the
permission of the copyright holders.

A catalogue record for this book is available from
the British Library

Produced by Toppan
Printed in China

CONTENTS

INTRODUCTION

I spend far more time than I really should in secondhand bookshops. Perhaps not surprisingly, it is generally the gardening sections that occupy most of my attention, and over the years I have accumulated a considerable library of Victorian gardening volumes. These are fascinating in themselves, because gardening techniques have changed greatly over the past 150 years or so – and there is nothing like the past for teaching you about the present. But an expression that crops up very rarely in the gardening literature of the nineteenth century is 'ground cover plant'. This is because although there have been low-growing plants as long as there have been plants of any kind, their use by gardeners in the way that we now understand the expression is a phenomenon that began in the second half of the twentieth century.

The development of the ground cover plant has gone hand-in-hand with the idea of wishing our gardens to be labour-saving. In the nineteenth century no one who owned a garden worthy of the name was short of either money or labour. Weeding, watering, feeding, pruning, cutting back and tidying up were all taken for granted as part of the stock-in-trade of the efficient running of any garden. Few gardens of substance were maintained in any significant measure by the people who owned them or made use of them for pleasure – but times change. Most gardens today are owner-maintained, and more time spent on maintenance means less time to spend on enjoyment or, indeed, on other, quite separate leisure activities. Hence the 'invention' of the ground cover plant, and on p. 6 I shall explain just how ground cover works and achieves the objectives.

There are no special families of ground

Ground cover plants can be used in many ways, both functional and aesthetic. Here they provide a delightful velvet carpet around paving

cover plants. Almost all belong to families or even genera that also contain tall, compact or even upright species. The range of plants I have described here, therefore, represents a considerable

number of families and, as with other books in this series, it is a selection based on my personal experience. It includes the plants that I expect you to find in the section labelled 'Ground Cover' at your local garden centre, as well as a number of others that I have found to perform well in this role. No doubt there are more that other gardeners have also found valuable.

There are some important points to make about my selection, nonetheless. I have included plants with a wide range of size and vigour, and you will need to take account of this when making your choice. The alpine plant that is an effective ground cover species in a small bed will be lost in a large one; similarly, a vigorous ground cover shrub will swamp a small plot almost overnight – so do check my size measurements carefully. I have also indicated which varieties have been awarded the Award of Garden Merit (AGM) of the Royal Horticultural Society. This doesn't necessarily mean that you will like them (there are some AGM plants that I loathe), but it does indicate that in trials assessed by experts they have been proved to be appropriate and good garden subjects.

The ability to suppress weed growth is almost always a primary reason for using ground cover (see p. 6), so for each plant type I have indicated how effectively this is achieved once the plant is fully established and mature, using a rating of 1 to 5 – 1 being fairly ineffective, 5 very effective – that, again, is based on my own experience.

Finally, do try not to confuse 'ground cover' with 'invasive'. An invasive plant (which, of course, need not necessarily be low growing) will spread very rapidly and may indeed then be difficult to eradicate. Some ground cover species undoubtedly are invasive (if they achieve their ground-covering effects very rapidly), and I have endeavoured to indicate this in my descriptions.

Campanula takesimana **suppresses weed growth around this stone bench and gives complementary colour too**

Vinca minor **'Gertrude Jekyll' is one of many invaluable ground cover plants to have been granted the Award of Garden Merit (AGM)**

PRINCIPLES OF GROUND COVER

You may want ground cover in your garden simply because of its aesthetic appeal. There is an undeniable attraction in what is known technically as a 'low-growing monoculture' ('monoculture' simply denoting a planting of only one type of plant). This, after all, is why for centuries gardeners have embellished large parts of their gardens with lawns. A lawn is a low-growing monoculture – or at least, it generally starts out as a monoculture but after a few years can end up as a mixed planting when daisies, speedwells, clovers, dandelions and other plants make their appearance within the turf! It's because of this appearance of other types of plant that grass lawns, despite their almost universal appeal, aren't ideal ground cover. Their popularity depends much more on the ability of grass to be walked on and mown than on its ability to suppress weeds.

Ground cover plants like this *Lamium maculatum* 'White Nancy' smother weed growth and help the soil to stay moist

How ground cover works

So what *does* constitute good ground cover, and how does it work? I've already described the use of ground cover as being appropriate for today's busy gardener, and I say this because it is a technique that enables you to maintain a relatively large area of your garden in a way that is significantly labour and trouble free. It is the embodiment of the concept of minimal maintenance. I've also often said that the ground cover concept is the classic gardening example of ecology in action.

The concept of ground cover is concerned principally with competition among plants and secondarily with the maintenance of soil moisture. By hugging the soil with an embracing carpet of foliage and stems, a low-growing ground cover plant denies light to others, most notably annual weeds, and so starves them out. It also limits water loss by evaporation from the soil surface and so maintains more moisture for the use of other plants growing nearby.

Weed suppression

However, to be effective a ground cover plant must be fairly fast growing, if not truly aggressive, and it thereby runs the risk of swamping not only weeds but also

Blending together ground cover plants of different types can produce strikingly attractive plantings

other garden plants. A very careful compromise is therefore required. I have just mentioned the use of ground cover to control annual weeds. These are relatively vulnerable to competition because they lack a major energy resource on which they can draw. They have small root systems and grow in a 'hand to mouth' manner: deny them light and air and there's nothing left. Perennial weeds are different, however. Denied light and air, they are able to draw on stored supplies of food and energy through their deep and extensive root systems. This isn't to say that they, too, can't be starved out by a vigorous ground cover plant, but it is undeniable that any ground cover plant vigorous enough to stand a fighting chance against perennial weeds will also all but devour any innocent herbaceous garden plants in the vicinity.

Never overlook the problem of what to do while the ground cover plant is itself growing and maturing. A seedling ground cover species will be vulnerable to competition in the early stages and must be cared for. It is a mistake to imagine that a young ground cover species is better able to cope with competition than any other plant. You should hand-weed carefully around your young ground cover plants therefore until they really are properly established. Don't use weedkillers which could damage them.

As already mentioned, in the Plant Directory a rating from 1 to 5 indicates how effective each plant type is at weed suppression. If this is your primary objective in growing ground cover plants, note this rating carefully – and note carefully, too, how easy it will be to hand-weed between the plants if they themselves are in category 3 or lower. Ground cover roses always seem to me to be the classic

Plants with large leaves or masses of tiny leaves will both produce effective ground cover

examples of plants that might look very pretty when sprawling across the ground, but in a weedy bed they will be counterproductive. Their fairly open texture means that they don't suppress weeds very well (I have put them in category 2) while, with few exceptions, their thorns prevent you from doing it.

USING GROUND COVER IN YOUR GARDEN

While most ornamental garden plants are grown solely for their attractive appearance, ground cover plants are slightly different. They are usually grown to satisfy the dual purposes of the aesthetic and the functional, so let's look now at the ways in which these two different roles can be combined.

Ground cover plants blend with many other types of garden plant. Because they are generally low growing, they are usually placed towards the front of borders, although types that grow fairly tall as well as spreading may be part of the middle-of-the-border plantings. Few ground cover species are likely to be placed at the back of mixed plantings.

Ground cover plants needn't prevent you growing bulbs, which will push their way through the ground cover

Good companions

In the early stages, before the ground is indeed fully covered, ground cover subjects may be interplanted with annuals, but once they become better established and more wide spreading the annuals will suffer the same fate as annual weeds and be completely suppressed – if indeed there is even sufficient space to plant them initially. Bulbs, on the other hand, may be planted with some types of ground cover, and I have seen some attractive combinations where shorter bulbs emerge through the stems of open-textured, deciduous ground cover shrubs to flower early in the season, before the ground cover foliage is present. Tall bulbs like daffodils seldom look right, however.

Ground cover plants are not appropriate for containers: even small varieties such as alpines will very swiftly swamp the entire planting, and it is a big mistake to plant them in alpine troughs, as happens all too often.

One type of ornamental bed that exemplified the way in which ground cover works but has (thankfully, in my view) now passed out of favour, was the conifer-and-heather bed. There, a ground cover planting of *Calluna*, *Erica* or *Daboecia* heathers was interplanted with medium-sized and tall-growing conifers. It showed what could be done and certainly required minimal maintenance, but unfortunately the limited range of foliage textures and the absence of flowers on the conifers meant that gardeners soon tired of it. Nevertheless, the conifer-and-heather bed did demonstrate the way to create a carpet of colour from which taller plants can emerge. A comparable theme could utilize plants like ornamental grasses, hardy geraniums, ivies or spreading perennials such as *Campanula glomerata* instead of the heathers, and

herbaceous perennials or flowering shrubs and trees instead of conifers. My own planting of *Stephanandra incisa* 'Crispa' with fastigiate trees (see p. 46) is another variation on this idea.

Function versus aesthetics

There will be areas, especially in large gardens, where the primary objective is not aesthetic but simply to keep matters under control with the minimum of attention, and here the rapid-growing, more invasive ground cover plants come into their own. Once they are established, the attention needed should be minimal for many years.

Paradoxically, ground cover plants can look extremely attractive in situations where their role of weed suppression and moisture retention is not especially relevant. Their low-growing habit is what matters here. Some of the most successful plantings in my gravel garden are of ground cover species such as ornamental grasses and shrubs like *Salix repens*, where the gravel itself (especially if it has an underlying impervious mat) suppresses the weeds and maintains soil moisture. Such an area might be the place to think about using any particularly attractive plants that fall below my weed suppression category 3, and this underlines the fact that gardeners need to keep an open mind when buying and using the plants that we call ground cover. Never forget that such plants have the dual capability of looking good and/or saving you work.

Just as with any other plants, it's important to blend colours in ground cover plantings with care

The ideal ground cover is one that looks attractive all year round

PLANTS AND PLANTING

You can obtain your plants in one of two ways: by buying them or by raising them yourself from seed. For most of the ground cover plants that I recommend in this book, buying them is likely to prove the best option. This is partly because the whole process will be speeded up and you will have something to plant immediately. But it's also because many of the plants are specially selected varieties that don't come true from seed and can be multiplied only by cuttings, division or even grafting.

Container versus bare-rooted

If you buy your plants from a garden centre, the chances are that they will be in containers: either container grown or containerized. A container-grown plant is one that has been in the container since it was planted there as a cutting or seedling; a containerized plant, on the other hand, has been grown in an open bed in the nursery, dug up and put in the container for sale. Although this is generally more of a problem with relatively large trees, a containerized shrub might just have incurred some damage to its roots in the course of being moved, and if your plant is a particularly large, rare or expensive one it would be worth checking on its origin.

If you buy a large shrub or purchase it by mail order (which will almost certainly be necessary for anything out of the ordinary), it will probably be delivered during the dormant period (winter to spring) and may well be bare-rooted or, at best, rootballed – that is, fairly loosely packed in organic matter, contained within a plastic bag. While a plant in a container can be planted at your leisure, a bare-

When planting a shrub, dig a hole about twice the volume of the compost ball. Mix the soil from the hole with organic material and bonemeal

rooted or rootballed one must be dealt with promptly and either planted in its permanent growing position or heeled in temporarily by simply unwrapping the plant, digging a shallow hole and covering the roots with soil.

Planting

Prepare the permanent planting position by digging a hole of approximately twice the volume of the ball of compost if the plant is in a container, or twice the root spread of a bare-rooted or rootballed plant. This is as true for a small alpine as it is for a large shrub – it's just the scale that is different. Mix the soil removed from the hole with a roughly equal volume of compost or similar organic matter, together with a few handfuls of bonemeal. This is rich in phosphate, which aids root development and will help the plant to establish quickly.

If the plant is a bare-rooted shrub, spread the roots carefully in the planting hole and cut off any that are wayward or crossing. Gently replace the soil and compost mixture in the hole, moving the plant up and down if necessary to ensure that no air pockets remain among the roots. I always like to tease away the roots lightly around the edge of the compost ball of a plant from a container as otherwise they tend to grow inwards, towards the generally more moist compost in the centre, rather than out into the surrounding soil. Firm the soil carefully with your hands or boot as you fill the hole but don't ram it down too hard. Finally, make sure that you finish by making a small mound with the soil sloping away from the plant's stem. This will prevent water from collecting at the base, freezing and causing damage. Water the plant thoroughly after planting and do keep the area immediately around the base free from competition with weeds. As I pointed out on p. 7, in its early stages a weed-suppressing ground cover plant is as vulnerable to competition as anything else.

Ground cover can be very effective on a miniature scale. *Mentha requienii* has some of the smallest leaves and flowers of any plant

CARE AND MAINTENANCE

Because ground cover plants must, by their nature, be able to compete very effectively with other plants, they respond particularly well to supplementary feeding and watering. However, the best fertilizer to use and the frequency with which it should be applied varies from plant to plant. To keep matters as simple as possible, I have suggested in most instances that your plants are fed once, at the start of the season, although I have recommended different fertilizers for those species that are grown primarily for their foliage effect and those that are grown to flower. It's useful to understand why this should be.

Feeding

For foliage ground cover plants, the most useful fertilizer will be a balanced general blend such as the organically based fish, blood and bone with an approximate nitrogen:potash:phosphate (N:P:K) ratio of 5:5:6, or a comparable artificial mixture, such as Growmore, with a ratio of 7:7:7, although I find the artificials to be rather too fast acting for optimum results and their benefits do not last long. It's worth a reminder that proprietary fish, blood and bone with the above composition is only organically *based*, not entirely organic as many gardeners seem to believe. This is because a mixture containing only fishmeal, dried blood and bonemeal would be deficient in potash, and so potassium sulphate is added to produce a more useful blend. Fertilizers such as these should be applied at the rate of a small handful scattered around each plant (a very small handful for alpines and other similar-sized species).

For flowering ground cover plants, you can also make do with a general fertilizer,

Minimal maintenance is an ideal attribute for ground cover, but *Euonymus fortunei* 'Sunspot' does need to be checked for any all-green shoots

but will usually obtain better results with one that contains proportionately more potash to encourage flowering. I use proprietary rose fertilizer, of which there are now both organic and artificial types.

There's not much point in simply dumping dry fertilizer powder around a ground cover plant growing in inherently dry soil, for it will remain on the surface, become caked and give no benefit to the plant.

Sometimes it's necessary to combine ground cover plants with organic mulch to achieve the objectives

Ideally, you should apply it after rain, rake it into the soil surface and then water it in with a watering can or hose.

Mulching

In order to try to maintain the soil around ground cover plants in a moist condition, you should apply a mulch in spring and again in autumn. But remember that the soil must be wet initially: a mulch will keep a dry soil dry just as much as it will keep a wet one wet. By and large, the most useful mulching material is home-produced garden compost or leaf mould, although acid-loving plants benefit from a mulch of chopped conifer needles. Once the plant is well established and, of course, covering the ground, applying a mulch will become difficult and the plant itself will take over this function – it becomes 'self-mulching'.

Pruning

Most ground cover plants should need little additional attention: after all, they are the embodiment of labour-saving gardening. In a few instances, however, some light pruning or trimming will be advantageous, and I have indicated this in the descriptions. More detailed information about pruning is given in my book *Best Pruning*, but it's worth making one or two points here.

Pruning entails cutting off parts of plants. Clearly, this reduces their size but, more importantly, it stimulates other parts to grow. The buds at the end or apex of a stem exert a suppressing influence on other buds further down. This suppressing effect can be reduced by bending vertical stems downwards, and this is done routinely with climbing shrubs to stimulate flower production over the whole plant. The phenomenon is called apical dominance, but in ground cover plants which tend naturally to grow horizontally, that apical dominance has already been suppressed so little or no interference on our part is needed.

It is still worth pruning away damaged or diseased shoots, however, and you should also keep an eye open for those shoots that show any tendency to grow vertically rather than horizontally; some of the ground cover conifers are rather prone to this. Plants with variegated foliage quite commonly produce some shoots with all-green leaves (the excellent ground cover variety of *Euonymus fortunei* called 'Sunspot' tends to do this). These shoots should be removed promptly, as they are invariably more vigorous than those with variegation and will gradually take over the plant.

Ground cover plants like ivy will very effectively soften hard surfaces and straight edges of benches and paths

PESTS AND DISEASES

Sooty mould on *Skimmia* foliage

Whiteflies can proliferate on the dense foliage of ground cover plants

Coral spot dieback on *Pyracantha*

Because ground cover plants are not a uniform, botanical grouping, we can't point to individual types of pest and disease to which they are likely to be especially subject. But if they aren't closely related in a botanical sense, the common habit features that make them so effective at covering the ground and suppressing weeds do mean that they are prone to any problem organism that will thrive among their close, dense foliage and twigs, and in the relatively greater warmth and moisture of the environment near to soil level.

Leaf-, flower-, bud- and fruit-attacking moulds, some types of mildew, rusts and decay fungi are therefore likely to be especially prevalent among diseases. Ground cover plants growing beneath overhanging trees may well accumulate sticky honeydew dripping from the foliage and this in is turn can give rise to black, sooty mould growth. Aphids are probably the most important pests, although red spider mites may be problematic in hot weather, and softer, herbaceous plants will attract the attention of woodlice, slugs and millepedes.

What I like to call 'garden hygiene' is particularly important in this close environment to help minimize damage. Wherever practicable, collect up fallen leaves and fruits from among ground cover plants and cut out dead, damaged or diseased shoots. As in other areas of gardening, the use of a chemical spray should be a last, not a first, resort, and only if you grow some of the older varieties of ground cover roses would I expect spraying ever to have to be a routine activity.

You will find more information on the recognition and control of garden pests and diseases in my book *Best Garden Doctor*, but I have given treatment advice here for the more common problems you are likely to encounter among ground cover species.

Treatments for common pest and disease problems on ground cover plants

Problem	Treatment	Problem	Treatment
Aphids (infesting leaves or shoots)	Use any proprietary contact insecticide; pick off affected shoots by hand or wash off insects with a hose.	**Red spider mite (bronzing of leaves; cobwebs)**	No treatment is really feasible, although keeping plants well watered and mulched will help limit the impact of attacks.
Beetles (holes in leaves)	Normally, treatment is not necessary or justified, but in cases of extensive attack use any proprietary contact insecticide.	**Root pest**	Normally, no treatment is feasible, but with severe and persistent attacks, dust around affected plants with derris or another soil insecticide.
Birds (eating fruit)	Erect netting or other protection; in really severe cases, erect bird scarers but remember that all birds enjoy legal protection and may not be harmed.	**Root disease/rot**	Destroy severely affected plants.
Canker (shrubs)	Cut out and destroy affected branches; no chemical treatment is possible.	**Rust**	Spray with penconazole fungicide.
		Scale insects	Spray with systemic insecticide.
Caterpillars (on foliage)	Pick off by hand if the caterpillars can be found and are present in small numbers. If masses of insects occur, pick off and destroy entire affected leaves or use any proprietary contact insecticide.	**Slugs**	Use proprietary slug pellets or liquid controls, or home-made remedies such as traps baited with beer. Surround the base of the plants with fine powders such as ash or soot, or a low barrier of finely spiny twigs such as gorse.
Coral spot dieback (shrubs)	Cut away and destroy affected branches or twigs, cutting well into the healthy wood. On valuable ornamental plants, spray the surrounding branches with a systemic fungicide.	**Snails**	If serious, use methods recommended for slugs, but generally they are less serious and fewer in number and can be combated by collecting them by hand and by locating and eradicating them from their hiding places among climbing plants.
Fireblight	Cut away and destroy affected branches. If the problem spreads, destroy plants.	**Sooty mould**	Wash off mould with water or destroy badly affected leaves, then identify and treat the insect pest responsible for the honeydew on which the mould grows.
Grey mould	Destroy affected parts; spray with systemic fungicide.		
Leaf miners	Remove and destroy affected leaves on herbaceous plants.	**Stem and foot rot**	Little can be done, but as it is often associated with waterlogging, improve drainage of the affected area.
Leaf spot	In most instances no treatment is necessary, for leaf spot diseases are rarely severe. Where attacks appear to be related to generally poor growth, however, spray with systemic fungicide.	**Vine weevil**	Adults feeding on leaves can be discouraged by mulching with organic material. Use proprietary biological control watered onto the soil to control root-attacking larvae.
Mice/voles	Set traps or used proprietary baits.	**Virus (disfigured foliage)**	Effects are usually mild, so no treatment is necessary.
Mildew	Ensure that plants are not allowed to become too dry and apply systemic fungicide or sulphur.	**Whiteflies**	No treatment is feasible on outdoor plants.
Millepedes	Dust affected areas with derris.	**Woodlice**	Dust around plants with a proprietary soil insecticide and locate and eradicate the pests from their hiding places.

SHRUBS

Arctostaphylos

6 6 *The bearberry is one of the ground cover shrubs most familiar to people who spend their leisure time walking remote upland hills, yet I doubt if more than one in a hundred could name it. Its garden status is comparable: generally unnoticed, but playing an important role (although do take note of its soil requirements). I'm sure that the common name must be a reference to the situation in some parts of the world where the fruit is eaten by bears.* 9 9

■ **CARE** Apart from its precise site and soil conditions, this shrub requires little attention.

■ **PROPAGATION** Take softwood cuttings in summer or lift some of the self-rooted layers that form readily from the parent plant.

■ **PRUNING** None.

■ **PROBLEMS** None.

■ **FEATURES** Evergreen, with small, bright green leaves and some red markings on the stems. In late spring or early summer white-tinted pink flowers hang like small bells over the plant. Small, round red fruits are produced in autumn.

Recommended varieties
Arctostaphylos nevadensis (pine-mat manzanita) prostrate Californian species that is only moderately hardy, tolerating about -15°C (5°F); *A. uva-ursi* (common bearberry) alpine shrub, 'Vancouver Jade', pink flowers.

Aucuba Spotted laurel

6 6 *I'm among an increasing group of gardeners who are trying to restore aucubas to popularity after many years of their being consigned to the category of humdrum and boring. My main concern in promoting them is because they are attractive and tolerate conditions of shade and dryness, but the fact that some are also good ground cover is an added bonus.* 9 9

■ **CARE** Little necessary, but for fruit production it is essential to plant both a female form and a male form (such as the true species) to ensure pollination.

■ **PROPAGATION** Take softwood cuttings in early summer or hardwood cuttings in a cold frame in autumn or winter.

■ **PRUNING** None necessary, but may be cut back as required to keep it within bounds.

SIZE Most reach about 1 x 1m (3 x 3ft) after 5 years, 4 x 3.5m (13 x 11ft) ultimately, but ground cover form recommended here rarely exceeds 1 x 1m (3 x 3ft).

SITE AND SOIL Valued for ability to withstand shade, pollution and extremes of soil conditions such as dryness or heavy clay.

Weed Suppression Rating 4.

HARDINESS Very hardy, tolerating at least -20°C (-4°F).

Arctostaphylos uva-ursi '**Vancouver Jade**'

SIZE 10–50cm x 50cm–1.5m (4–20in x 20in–5ft).

SITE AND SOIL Acid soil in full sun essential, as will not tolerate alkaline soil, shade or waterlogging. Ideal for acidic gardens and excellent for colonizing a sandy bank, where it will tolerate the poor, dry soil.

Weed Suppression Rating 3.

HARDINESS Most are hardy, tolerating -15 to -20°C (5 to -4°F).

■ **PROBLEMS** None serious, although an unexplained blackening of the shoot tips is quite common.

■ **FEATURES** Tough evergreens for problem sites. Foliage may be plain green with either oval or pointed leaves, but many varieties are splashed with cream or yellow markings. Female forms have round fruits, usually red.

Recommended varieties
Aucuba japonica 'Nana Rotundifolia' small round shrub, small deep green leaves that have a sharp tooth near the tip, a freely fruiting female form but requires a male nearby.

Berberis Barberry

" *Ask any garden centre manager and they will tell you that the many species of* Berberis *are now among the most popular ornamental shrubs. They offer a wide range of flower and foliage features and are available in a considerable number of different growth habits. Their value as ground cover, however, is much less widely appreciated.* "

■ **CARE** Apply rose fertilizer in spring and midsummer to help promote flowering.

■ **PROPAGATION** Sow seed of species in autumn. Take semi-ripe cuttings of evergreen forms in early autumn.

■ **PRUNING** None necessary.

■ **PROBLEMS** None.

■ **FEATURES** Evergreen or deciduous shrubs, but for ground cover the evergreen forms are more useful. They have oval to elongated leaves in varying shades of green, some (unusually for evergreens) offering good autumn colour. Yellow or orange flowers appear in spring or early summer, often followed by dark fruits.

SIZE Varies, but forms recommended here reach 75 x 75cm (30 x 30in) after 5 years, 1.2–1.5 x 1.2–1.5m (4–5 x 4–5ft) after 10 years.
SITE AND SOIL Fairly sheltered site in light shade or sun. Thrives in most garden soils except very dry, and usefully tolerant of fairly heavy conditions.
Weed Suppression Rating 3.
HARDINESS Hardy to very hardy, most tolerating at least -20°C (-4°F).

Berberis verruculosa

Recommended varieties
Berberis x *bristolensis* small dense evergreen, small prickly leaves, foliage glossy green, white beneath, yellow flowers, blue-black fruits; *B. calliantha* AGM small evergreen, holly-like leaves with blue-green undersides, young stems crimson, pale yellow flowers, blue-black fruits; *B. candidula* dense, dome-shaped evergreen, small dark green leaves, white beneath, bright yellow flowers, white-purple fruits; *B. verruculosa* AGM compact evergreen, oval, spiny olive-green leaves, silver beneath, semi-double yellow flowers, blue-black fruits; *B. wilsoniae* AGM deciduous but almost evergreen, dense habit, thorny stems, grey-green foliage with autumn tints, yellow flowers in early summer, orange-red fruits.

SHRUBS

Buxus Box

❝ *There are several instances in this book where I recommend as ground cover a plant more familiar as a hedge. But while low-growing rather than upright varieties are required for ground cover, the same dense foliage is an attribute of importance for both roles. Box offers one of the best examples of this.* ❞

■ **CARE** Mulch and apply general fertilizer in spring.

■ **PROPAGATION** Take semi-ripe cuttings in summer or hardwood cuttings in autumn.

■ **PRUNING** Clip in midsummer and then again in mid-autumn; box will regenerate from old wood but not nearly as effectively as yew.

■ **PROBLEMS** Box aphids, whiteflies, box suckers, especially at times of the year when soft growth is produced in quantity; soft young shoots are prone to damage from late frosts.

■ **FEATURES** Tough, small-leaved evergreens that are very long lived.

SIZE In practice, usually clipped to much less than its natural size; box edging, for example, is often kept at 15–30 x 15–30cm (6–12 x 6–12in).
SITE AND SOIL Very tolerant of all soils including alkaline, but may suffer leaf scorch in sunny, dry sites. Valuable for ability to tolerate shade.
Weed Suppression Rating 5.
HARDINESS Very hardy, tolerating at least -20°C (-4°F).

Often grown as hedging, box may also be planted in blocks for ground cover effect.

Recommended varieties
There are many varieties, but the following are the best for ground cover: *Buxus microphylla* (small-leaved box) slow-growing, rounded shrub, dark green foliage turning bronze in winter, 40 x 75cm (16 x 30in) after 5 years, ultimately 1 x 1m (3 x 3ft), 'Compacta' very compact dense form, retains its bun shape without clipping, 30 x 30cm (12 x 12in); *B. sempervirens* 'Prostrata' (syn. 'Horizontalis') form of the common box with horizontally spreading branches, very variable in size but generally up to about 1.5–3m (5–10ft) across.

Buxus microphylla 'Compacta'

Calluna Heather

❝ *Assessed purely on the basis of the area of soil that is covered, heather must be one of the most effective ground cover shrubs in the northern hemisphere. This is, of course, because it naturally covers vast swathes of wild moorland. In gardens, its role is much less evident, but in wilder places with acidic soils it is no less effective.* ❞

■ **CARE** Mulch with an acidic mulch, such as chopped conifer needles, and apply rose fertilizer in spring.

■ **PROPAGATION** Take short semi-ripe cuttings in early summer; mounding soil in the middle of an old clump will result in a mass of fresh new growths, which may be used as cuttings. Can also be layered effectively.

■ **PRUNING** Regular clipping is worthwhile as plants soon become unkempt if left unpruned. Use single-

---

SIZE Varies greatly: short 15–25 x 30–50cm (6–10 x 12–20in); medium 30–35 x 40–50cm (12–14 x 16–20in); tall 40–50 x 50–70cm (16–20 x 20-28in). All these after 5 years, as best treated as short lived.
SITE AND SOIL Always best in full sun but tolerates light shade. Acidic, free-draining soil essential (for alkaline soils, choose appropriate varieties of *Erica* on p. 27). Excellent for windy, exposed gardens.
Weed Suppression Rating 5.
HARDINESS Very hardy, tolerating at least -20°C (-4°F).

handed shears after flowering or in early spring.

■ **PROBLEMS** Root rot may be a problem in wet soils; stem dieback may also occur.

■ **FEATURES** Evergreens with small leaves, the leaf colour changing attractively through the seasons. Masses of tiny, dainty flowers in shades of mauve, red, pink or white are produced in summer.

Ceanothus thyrsiflorus var. *repens*

Ceanothus Californian lilac

❝ Ceanothus *is one of the most important garden shrubs because of its glorious flowers in a shade of blue that is particularly uncommon among easily grown species. Most have an upright habit, but there are a few low-growing forms that bring their floral features down to soil level in an even more unusual manner.* ❞

■ **CARE** Mulch in spring and apply rose fertilizer after pruning.
■ **PROPAGATION** Take semi-ripe cuttings in summer.
■ **PRUNING** Trim back lightly each year after flowering. Some damage from winter cold may be expected and should be cut out in spring.
■ **PROBLEMS** Leaves may show signs of chlorosis on thin, alkaline soils.
■ **FEATURES** Evergreen and decidu-

ous shrubs, but only a few low-growing evergreen species are suitable as ground cover. Leaves are small and dark green, but the main attraction is the clouds of massed tiny blue flowers in late spring or early summer.

Cistus Rock rose, Sun rose

“ *The sight of* Cistus *growing in a garden, even on a dull day, almost instantly conjures up images of the hot, sun-baked hillsides of the Mediterranean that are their home. You can almost smell their natural accompaniment of pine trees and herbs. They are wonderfully light and airy looking plants and are among the species that straddle the boundary between herbaceous plants and shrubs; sub-shrubs is a useful term for them.* ”

■ **CARE** Apply general fertilizer in spring and summer. Dead-head to encourage flowering. In colder areas, give some winter protection with mulch and straw, bracken or similar wrapping to the crown.

■ **PROPAGATION** Take semi-ripe cuttings in summer or hardwood cuttings in winter. Some species may be raised from seed sown in autumn.

■ **PRUNING** Little necessary; cut away winter-damaged shoots in spring but avoid cutting into old wood.

■ **PROBLEMS** None, if they are sited correctly to avoid shade, wet clay soils and cold winds.

■ **FEATURES** Evergreens, those recommended here having dark green leaves. Saucer-shaped flowers, usually white and often with attractive dark markings, appear in early to mid-summer. Although the individual blooms are short lived, the flowers are produced in abundance.

SIZE Short lived, reaching 60cm-1m x 1–1.5m (2–3ft x 3–5ft) after 5 years.

SITE AND SOIL Full sun and shelter from cold essential, and light, free-draining soil. Ideal for sunny, sandy banks, rock gardens or mild coastal gardens.

Weed Suppression Rating 2.

HARDINESS Most are barely hardy to fairly hardy, tolerating -5 to -10°C (23 to 14°F).

Recommended varieties
There are many species and hybrids, but only the following are dense or spreading enough to be considered successful as ground cover: *Cistus* x *aguilarii* large bright green leaves, white flowers with yellow centres, 1 x 1.5m (3 x 5ft); *C.* x *dansereaui* 'Decumbens' AGM low, spreading habit, large white flowers with crimson blotch, 60cm x 1.2m (2 x 4ft); *C.* x *hybridus* (syns. *C.* x *corbariensis*, *C. coeris*) AGM dense habit, one of the hardiest (but still only fairly hardy), white flowers with yellow blotches open from red buds, 1 x 1m (3 x 3ft).

Cistus x *dansereaui* 'Decumbens'

Coprosma

❝ It's hard to become excited about coprosmas, and although they have a certain individual charm, I can't believe they will ever win many prizes (there certainly isn't an AGM among the many species). But in milder gardens especially, their tiny leaves mass together to create rather effective ground cover. ❞

■ **CARE** Mulch and apply general fertilizer in spring. Give protection in the first winter after planting, and in colder areas place in a sheltered position.
■ **PROPAGATION** Sow seed in early spring or take semi-ripe cuttings in midsummer.
■ **PRUNING** None necessary.
■ **PROBLEMS** None.
■ **FEATURES** Evergreens grown for their foliage, as the small flowers are inconspicuous. Attractive fruits in late summer or autumn if male and female plants are grown together.

SIZE Varies greatly (see Recommended varieties).
SITE AND SOIL Well-drained soil in full sun.
Weed Suppression Rating 3.
HARDINESS Moderately hardy, tolerating -10 to -15°C (14 to 5°F).

Recommended varieties
Coprosma propinqua wiry-stemmed shrub from New Zealand, female plants bearing blue fruits if there are males nearby, 3 x 3m (10 x 10ft).

Cornus Dogwood

❝ Cornus canadensis *is an oddity among dogwoods: it is almost a herbaceous plant and very different from the shrubs that we grow for their brightly coloured winter stems. I find it isn't always easy to establish, but having been fortunate enough to see it clothing the ground of huge areas of native forest in the Canadian Rockies, I know that persistence will eventually be well rewarded.* ❞

■ **CARE** Mulch with leaf mould in autumn and early spring, and apply rose fertilizer in spring.
■ **PROPAGATION** Lift and divide in autumn or early spring as you would a herbaceous perennial, or layer in spring.
■ **PRUNING** None necessary.
■ **PROBLEMS** None.
■ **FEATURES** Soil-hugging relative of the more familiar dogwoods that makes good woodland ground cover. It is semi-evergreen with rounded, fresh green leaves that develop red tints in autumn. In summer eye-catching white bracts appear around tiny green-purple flowers, which in turn are followed by bright red fruits.

SIZE 20 x 60cm (8 x 24in) after 5 years, ultimately 20cm x 3–4m (8in x 10–13ft).
SITE AND SOIL Light to moderate shade. Tolerates a wide range of soils but spreads best in well-drained, acidic loam; not really successful on heavy clays.
Weed Suppression Rating 4.
HARDINESS Hardy, tolerating -15 to -20°C (5 to -4°F).

Recommended varieties
Cornus canadensis (syn. *Chamaepericlymenum canadense*) (creeping dogwood) AGM only the true species is available.

Cornus canadensis

Cotoneaster

“ *The genus* Cotoneaster *occupies a rather special place in gardening, although it does fall into the category of shrubs that are still taken too much for granted and whose real merit isn't fully recognized. I feel this is typically borne out by the number of times someone asks me the name of a plant that has appealed to them and are then greatly surprised to discover that it is, indeed, yet another cotoneaster that has taken their eye. There are around 70 species, with a considerable range of varieties among some of them. They are northern temperate plants with a rather wide distribution, including many from distinctly cold places, so the majority are fully hardy. A large number, including many deciduous species, form extremely effective ground cover, and those I recommend here are simply some that I have grown. You may well find others that will perform the role with comparable effectiveness.* ”

SIZE Low-growing forms reach about 50cm x 1m (20in x 3ft) after 5 years, 1 x 2m (3 x 6ft) after 10 years.
SITE AND SOIL Full sun to moderate shade. Thrives in any reasonable garden soil but least successful on shallow, dry, alkaline sites. Ideal for windy, exposed gardens.
Weed Suppression Rating 3–4.
HARDINESS Very hardy, tolerating at least -20°C (-4°F).

■ **CARE** Little necessary, but benefits from general or rose fertilizer in spring.
■ **PROPAGATION** Take semi-ripe cuttings in summer or hardwood cuttings in winter. Some low-growing forms may be layered.
■ **PRUNING** None needed, although if it becomes necessary to restrict the height, light pruning should be performed in spring.

■ **PROBLEMS** Fireblight.
■ **FEATURES** Deciduous or evergreen shrubs with dark to grey-green foliage, some with late-season colour due to the red coloration displayed by the older leaves. White blossom is borne in spring or early summer, followed by fruits in autumn. There are wide variations in habit among the different species.

Cotoneaster dammeri

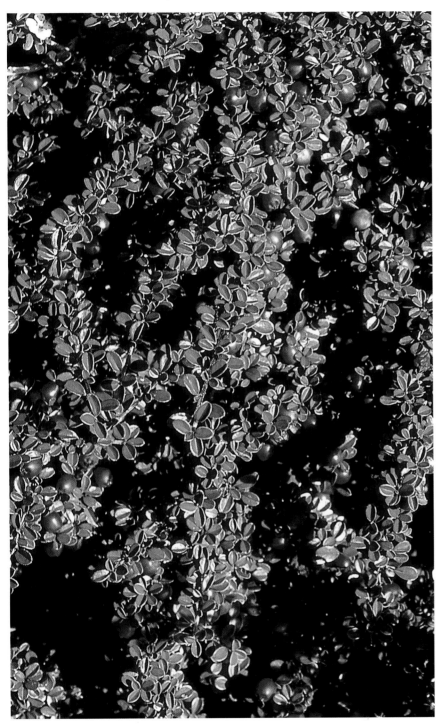

Cotoneaster microphyllus var. cochleatus

Recommended varieties

Cotoneaster adpressus AGM deciduous, prostrate shrub, good autumn colour, 30cm x 2m (12in x 6ft); *C. congestus* (syn. *C. pyrenaicus*) evergreen, dense, creeping habit, 10–70 x 90cm (4–28 x 36in), 'Nanus' ideal for rock gardens as only 5 x 50cm (2 x 20in); *C. conspicuus* 'Decorus' AGM evergreen, low growing with arching habit, ideal for banks, 20cm x 1.2m (8in x 4ft); *C. dammeri* AGM evergreen, prostrate, stems root into the soil, dark green to red foliage, 5–20cm x 1.2–2m (2–8in x 4–6ft); *C. horizontalis* (fishbone cotoneaster) AGM deciduous, spreading branches make a herringbone pattern, autumn colour, 30 x 60cm (12 x 24in), then 60–90cm x 1.5–2m (24–36in x 5–6ft); *C. microphyllus* AGM evergreen, low-growing mound, large red fruits, 30cm x 1m (12in x 3ft), then 75cm x 1m (30in x 3ft), plants sold under this name can be *C. integrifolius*, which has dark pink fruits and is 1 x 1.5m (3 x 5ft); *C. nanshan* (syn. *C. adpressus* var. *praecox*) deciduous, dwarf shrub with arching branches, good autumn colour, pink-red flush to white flowers, large orange-red fruits, 1 x 2m (3 x 6ft); *C. salicifolius* 'Parkteppich' evergreen with scrambling habit, 'Pendulus' (syn. *C.* 'Hybridus Pendulus') often sold grafted to form a weeping standard but natural habit is ground cover, when it is 60cm x 2m (24in x 6ft), 'Repens' prostrate form; *C.* x *suecicus* 'Coral Beauty' evergreen with arching branches, coral-red fruits, 25–60cm x 1.2m (10–24in x 4ft).

SHRUBS

Cytisus Broom

❝ I suppose it is the extremely small size of their leaves that in theory would tend to rule out brooms as good smothering plants. Like many another small-leaved shrub, however, the leaves are so numerous and the stems so closely massed that they fill the role with both effectiveness and charm. ❞

■ **CARE** No special care necessary if the site and soil are right, but these are short-lived shrubs so it is worth propagating a few cuttings in order to have stock available to replace old plants.

■ **PROPAGATION** Take semi-ripe cuttings in late summer, pinching out the growing tips when young plants are 25cm (10in) high to ensure bushy growth. Species may be raised from seed sown in spring.

■ **PRUNING** Best left unpruned, but may be lightly trimmed after flowering, taking care not to cut into old wood.

■ **PROBLEMS** None.

■ **FEATURES** Deciduous plants, ranging from prostrate shrubs to small trees. Leaves are tiny and unremarkable, but the main feature is the small, pea-like flowers, which smother the plants in late spring or early summer.

SIZE Low-growing forms generally reach 20-60cm x 1–1.5m (8–24in x 3–5ft) after 5 years. Short lived, becoming leggy after 10 years or so.
SITE AND SOIL Full sun essential. Well-drained soil (ideal for sandy soils), although most reasonable garden soils will do, but avoid very fertile soils.
Weed Suppression Rating 2–3.
HARDINESS Moderately hardy to hardy, tolerating -15°C (5°F).

Recommended varieties
Cytisus ardoinoi AGM hummock-like shrub, bright yellow flowers, 10–20 x 30–60cm (4-8 x 12–24in); *C. x beanii* AGM golden yellow flowers, 30 x 60cm (12 x 24in), then 60cm x 1m (24 x 3ft); *C. decumbens* (syn. *Genista decumbens*) prostrate habit with wiry, branching stems, brilliant yellow flowers, 10–30cm x 1m (4–12in x 3ft); *C. x kewensis* AGM prostrate habit with arching stems, pale yellow to cream flowers, 30cm x 1.5m (1 x 5ft); *C. scoparius* subsp. *maritimus* low-growing form of the common broom, large yellow flowers, ideal for mild coastal gardens, 20cm x 1.5m (8in x 5ft).

Daboecia

❝ On more than one occasion, I've called Daboecia *the 'forgotten' heather. It is certainly the least well known of the trio that also includes* Calluna *and* Erica*, but its flowers are better than almost any. ❞*

■ **CARE** Plant deeply and water well for the first growing season.

■ **PROPAGATION** Take shoot-tip cuttings in summer or layer like other heathers.

■ **PRUNING** Prune annually, cutting back to the base of the dead flowers in spring.

■ **PROBLEMS** Unsuitable soil and root rot are the main problems.

■ **FEATURES** Evergreen foliage comprising glossy, dark green leaves with white undersides. Small, hanging purple-pink or white flowers bloom in early summer and again in autumn.

Cytisus x kewensis

Daboecia cantabrica 'Atropurpurea'

SIZE 40 x 70cm (16 x 28in) after 5 years; plants are short lived and best replaced after 5–7 years.
SITE AND SOIL Acidic or neutral soil with plenty of humus, producing moist but well-drained conditions. Thrives in an open site in sun or light shade, but unsuccessful in frost pockets. Grow between dwarf conifers or acid-loving shrubs.
Weed Suppression Rating 4–5.
HARDINESS *Daboecia cantabrica* is hardy, tolerating -15 to -20°C (5 to -4°F), other species less so.

Recommended varieties
Daboecia cantabrica (Irish Heath, St Dabeoc's Heath) hardy species, lavender flowers, plus many named forms with differently coloured flowers: white (f. *alba*, 'David Moss' AGM, 'Snowdrift'), rose-purple ('Atropurpurea', 'Hookstone Purple', 'Porter's Variety', 'Waley's Red'), white, pink and red ('Bicolor' AGM).

Dryas Mountain avens

6 6 *I can think of three garden plant genera (*Banksia, Dryandra *and* Hydrangea*) with a species called* quercifolia, *meaning oak-leaved. It's long been a mystery to me why* Dryas *isn't one of them, because few plants have leaves more like an oak tree than these. On the other hand, nor are many more unlike an oak in habit, this lovely if rather woody alpine having an extremely low-growing, soil-hugging habit.* 9 9

■ **CARE** Easy to grow, but if the soil is at all heavy dig in grit to improve the drainage before planting.
■ **PROPAGATION** Take semi-ripe cuttings in summer. Sow ripe seed in late summer or autumn. Lift and transplant rooted stems in spring.
■ **PRUNING** None necessary.
■ **PROBLEMS** None.

■ **FEATURES** Prostrate and evergreen, with a mat of oak-like leaves. Large white flowers appear from late spring to early summer and are followed by decorative seedheads.

SIZE 10–20 x 60–90cm (4–8 x 24–36in) after 5 years.
SITE AND SOIL Full sun and well-drained soil essential. Ideal for covering a large sunny rock garden or front of a border.
Weed Suppression Rating 4.
HARDINESS Very hardy, tolerating -20°C (-4°F)

Recommended varieties
There are only a few species and the following is much the best for ground cover: *Dryas octopetala* AGM glossy green leaves with scalloped edges, white flowers with yellow centres, fluffy seedheads in autumn, 20 x 60cm (8 x 24in).

Dryas octopetala

SHRUBS

Empetrum

" *If the bearberry (see p. 16) was once eaten by bears, presumably the fruits of the crowberry (*Empetrum nigrum*), which grows in similar places, are eaten by crows. They are certainly striking, black and glossy and sit like pieces of polished jet on the mat of foliage; perhaps the name simply means they are the colour of crows.* "

■ **CARE** Little necessary, although a light application of rose fertilizer in spring will encourage flower and fruit formation.
■ **PROPAGATION** Take softwood cuttings in summer or hardwood cuttings in autumn; also comes true from seed sown in autumn.
■ **PRUNING** None necessary.

■ **PROBLEMS** None.
■ **FEATURES** Dwarf, carpeting evergreens with insignificant flowers but striking glossy black fruits.

SIZE 25–30 x 25–30cm (10–12 x 10–12in).
SITE AND SOIL Occurs naturally in high, exposed places so ideal for windy sites. Moist, acidic or neutral soil essential; unsuitable for alkaline sites.
Weed Suppression Rating 3.
HARDINESS Very hardy, tolerating -20°C (-4°F)

Recommended varieties
Empetrum nigrum (crowberry) widespreading, dense carpet, inconspicuous purple-red flowers, glossy black fruits.

Ephedra

" *Not many gardeners are likely to consider* Ephedra *a thing of great beauty, although it does have its fans and I count myself among them. This is more because of its decidedly odd appearance than its aesthetic charm, however. Grow it and I guarantee that the first visitor to your garden will ask its name.* "

■ **CARE** Apply general fertilizer in spring.
■ **PROPAGATION** Sow seed of hardy species in autumn in a cold frame. Lift and divide plants in spring or autumn.
■ **PRUNING** None necessary.
■ **PROBLEMS** None.
■ **FEATURES** Evergreen shrubs with a curious and fascinating appearance, as they provide a link between flowering shrubs and conifers and superficially look rather like *Equisetum*. Slender, rush-like green stems have their leaves reduced to tiny scales. The striking red fruits that appear on female plants are an additional attraction.

SIZE Variable and unaccountably so; plants may be procumbent or up to 1–2 x 1m (3–6 x 3ft), but invariably fairly wide spreading.
SITE AND SOIL Full sun and light, free-draining soil.
Weed Suppression Rating 1–2.
HARDINESS Forms recommended here are moderately hardy to hardy, tolerating at least -10°C (14°F).

Empetrum nigrum

Ephedra distachya

Recommended varieties
Ephedra americana var. *andina* usually a procumbent shrub, bright green, spreading shoots, red fruits; *E. distachya* (European shrubby horsetail) dwarf shrub, red fruits.

Erica Heather, Heaths

" Having given Calluna *(see p. 18) one of the top positions in respect of hectares of ground covered, I'm sure that its relative* Erica *must come second. To me, this is a much more attractive genus, however, because its flowers are so much larger. And it has the special advantage of including species that are tolerant of alkaline soils. "*

■ **CARE** Mulch with an acidic material such as pine needles. Most may be given a general or rose fertilizer in spring.

■ **PROPAGATION** Take short semi-ripe cuttings in early summer; mounding soil in the middle of an old clump will result in a mass of fresh new growths, which can be used as cuttings. May also be layered effectively.

SIZE Most reach their full size of 30–50 x 50–75cm (12–20 x 20–30in) within 3 years.
SITE AND SOIL Full sun to partial shade. Free-draining, acidic soil for most forms. Use *E. carnea* and *E.* x *darleyensis* where soil is alkaline, or grow acid-loving forms in containers of lime-free compost. Ideal for exposed sites.
Weed Suppression Rating 5.
HARDINESS Forms recommended here are hardy, tolerating -15 to -20°C (5 to -4°F).

Erica x *darleyensis* **varieties**

■ **PRUNING** Regular clipping is worthwhile as plants soon become unkempt if left. Use single-handed shears after flowering or in early spring.
■ **PROBLEMS** None.
■ **FEATURES** Evergreens with narrow, needle-like leaves in colourful shades of green or yellow, many developing winter tints. Small flowers (but larger than those of *Calluna*) are usually in shades of pink, purple, red or white.

Recommended varieties
The following entries indicate the range of flower and foliage colours you are likely to find, but there are so many varieties and their availability changes so rapidly that it is best to make your choice from those found at your garden centre or nursery: *Erica carnea* (syn. *E. herbacea*) varieties are winter-flowering heathers that tolerate lime; foliage is often orange-yellow with red tints in winter or spring, but some varieties have bright green or deep green-bronze foliage; flower colour varies from deep red, through various shades of pink, to white. *E.* x *darleyensis* varieties flower between winter and spring and are moderately lime tolerant; foliage tends to be green, often with cream or pink tips in spring, but yellow-orange foliage varieties are also available; flowers are usually in various shades of pink. *E. vagans* varieties require acidic soil; foliage is usually green and the summer to autumn flowers are white or in shades of pink.

Euonymus

❝ *Superficially,* Euonymus *seems to have too open and upright a habit to make good ground cover, but while this might be true of some species,* E. fortunei *produces such a dense mass of intertwining stems that in reality it is very effective. And it does have one of the most appealing leaf variegations.* ❞

■ **CARE** No special care necessary, but benefits from a general fertilizer in spring.

■ **PROPAGATION** Take softwood cuttings in early summer.

■ **PRUNING** Remove misplaced shoots and congested branches in spring and cut out all-green shoots on variegated forms.

■ **PROBLEMS** None.

■ **FEATURES** The best for ground cover is *E. fortunei* and its varieties. They are colourful trailing evergreens whose leaves have very striking white or gold variegations. Adult plants produce inconspicuous flowers in early summer and these are followed by pink

> **SIZE** Grown as ground cover, *E. fortunei* reaches 50–60cm x 2m (20–24in x 6ft) after 5 years, then continues to spread slowly to 3m (10ft), but many named varieties are smaller.
> **SITE AND SOIL** Full sun to partial or moderate shade. Any garden soil, including alkaline.
> **Weed Suppression Rating 4.**
> **HARDINESS** Hardy, tolerating -15 to -20°C (5 to -4°F).

fruits containing orange seeds, although in cooler climates these are produced only after hot summers.

> **Recommended varieties**
> *Euonymus fortunei* small, oval, glossy foliage, 'Emerald Gaiety' AGM rounded, grey-green foliage with white edges, pink tints in winter, 1 x 1.5m (3 x 5ft), 'Emerald 'n' Gold' AGM grey-green foliage with gold edges, pink tints in winter, 'Silver Queen' AGM foliage creamy yellow when young, later green with a white edge, pink tints in winter, 'Sunspot' (syn. 'Gold Spot') deep green foliage with a yellow blotch, red tints in winter, yellow stems.

Gaultheria

❝ *The fact that there is a species of* Gaultheria *called partridge berry should betray the fact that these plants provide very effective game cover. And a plant whose growth is dense enough to hide a flock of partridges is likely to be rather good at hiding other things, too. It's a pity, though, that they just aren't more attractive.* ❞

■ **CARE** Ensure that the roots do not dry out in summer by applying an acidic mulch such as conifer needles in spring.

■ **PROPAGATION** Take semi-ripe cuttings in autumn. If the plant is a suckering species, these may be removed for replanting.

■ **PRUNING** None necessary.

■ **PROBLEMS** None, but dig or pull out any unwanted suckers.

■ **FEATURES** Small, leathery dark green leaves and bell-shaped, white flowers, usually borne from late spring to early summer. The main attraction is the display of very striking and showy spherical fruit in pink, red, blue, purple or white that appear in autumn and last through the winter.

> **SIZE** Ground cover forms reach about 1 x 1.5m (3 x 5ft) after 5 years, but *G. procumbens* has a creeping habit.
> **SITE AND SOIL** Sun or partial shade. Acidic soil, moist in summer but well drained in winter.
> **Weed Suppression Rating 2–3.**
> **HARDINESS** Moderately hardy, tolerating -10 to -15°C (14 to 5°F).

Gaultheria x *wisleyensis* 'Wisley Pearl'

Recommended varieties

G. procumbens (wintergreen, partridge berry) AGM creeping species, glossy, dark green foliage, pink-white flowers in mid- to late summer followed by dark red fruits, 15 x 90cm (6 x 36in); *G. shallon* (salal, shalon) tolerates deep shade and forms a vigorous thicket, white flowers tinted with pink in late spring to early summer, red to dark purple fruits in autumn; *G.* x *wisleyensis* (syn. x *Gaulnettya wisleyensis*) bushy habit, white flowers in late spring early summer, red fruits, 'Wisley Pearl', similar but with deep red fruits.

Genista Broom, Gorse

❝ *The names broom and gorse are applied to a number of different but related plants in the pea family. Certainly, if you want low-growing plants with some of the most vivid yellow flowers, you will find your answer among one or other of these genera; and best of all, I think, in this one.* ❞

■ **CARE** No special care necessary, but benefits from general or rose fertilizer in spring.

■ **PROPAGATION** Take semi-ripe cuttings in late summer. Sow seed of species in autumn.

■ **PRUNING** Lightly trim or clip after flowering, but do not cut into old wood as this may encourage dieback. *G. lydia* should not be pruned.

■ **PROBLEMS** None.

■ **FEATURES** Deciduous shrubs, with masses of small, sweet pea-like, yellow

flowers in late spring to early summer. Foliage, usually green or grey-green, is small and hidden by the flowers which are produced in remarkable profusion.

> **SIZE** Forms recommended here reach 10–30 x 30–60cm (4–12 x 12–24in) after 5 years, some spreading to 1m (3ft) after 10 years.
> **SITE AND SOIL** Full sun essential, but any well-drained soil is suitable.
> **Weed Suppression Rating 3.**
> **HARDINESS** Moderately hardy, tolerating -10 to -15°C (14 to 5°F).

Recommended varieties

Genista hispanica (Spanish gorse) low, prickly bush, tolerates dry, sunny sites with poor soil; *G. lydia* AGM forms low mounds and is covered with masses of striking yellow flowers, a very good plant; *G. pilosa* (hairy greenweed) dwarf shrub, 'Goldilocks' vigorous upright branches reaching up to 60cm (24in), long flowering, 'Procumbens' forms a prostrate mat 60cm (24in) across, 'Yellow Spreader' a low mound, lemon-yellow flowers.

Genista pilosa 'Goldilocks'

SHRUBS

Halimium

❝ Any plant with a name that begins with 'Hali-' is likely to be coastal in origin, the word originating in the Greek for marine (and hence the term halophyte, a salt-loving plant). Halimium is a close relative of Helianthemum and Cistus and is a common seaside genus around the Mediterranean. You don't need to give it salt in your garden, but a light soil and a sunny position certainly won't go amiss. ❞

■ **CARE** In colder areas, give protection over winter and avoid frost pockets or other cold places for planting.

■ **PROPAGATION** Take semi-ripe cuttings in summer.

■ **PRUNING** To encourage flowering, cut back shoots by two-thirds in late summer but avoid cutting back into old wood.

Halimium lasianthum

■ **PROBLEMS** None, provided that the growing conditions are correct.

■ **FEATURES** Evergreen, with small, grey-green leaves. Saucer-shaped flowers of yellow or white appear in early to midsummer.

SIZE Up to 1 x 1.5m (3 x 5ft) after 5 years.

SITE AND SOIL Sunny, sheltered site and well-drained, sandy soil. Ideal ground cover for mild coastal gardens.

Weed Suppression Rating 2.

HARDINESS Barely hardy to fairly hardy, tolerating -5°C (23°F).

Recommended varieties

Halimium lasianthum (syn. *H. formosum, Cistus formosus, C. lasianthus*) AGM spreading shrub, golden flowers with a crimson blotch.

Hebe

❝ Hebes originate very largely from New Zealand, and although parts of the country can at times be cold and inhospitable, most of its plants find European winters rather hard going. Hebes are no exception, and valuable as some of them are, you must choose your species carefully if they are to survive in the long term. ❞

■ **CARE** No special care necessary, but some forms should be renewed regularly from cuttings.

■ **PROPAGATION** Take semi-ripe cuttings in late summer.

■ **PRUNING** None necessary, but

may be trimmed lightly after flowering.

■ **PROBLEMS** Leaf spot and associated shoot dieback, plus downy mildew in damp conditions.

■ **FEATURES** Evergreens in a range of sizes, leaf colours and textures. Some have attractive flowers in summer.

SIZE Varies greatly (see Recommended varieties), but full size is usually reached within 5 years.

SITE AND SOIL Full sun essential, but most soils are satisfactory provided they do not become waterlogged in winter. Ideal for coastal areas or other windy but mild sites.

Weed Suppression Rating 4.

HARDINESS Varies considerably and species should be selected carefully; most forms recommended here are moderately hardy, tolerating -10 to -15°C (14 to 5°F).

Hebe pinguifolia

Hedera Ivy

❝ *Love it or loathe it (and there are gardeners who do both), ivy can't be ignored. And if you want something that will cover the ground and suppress pretty well everything else, then ivy will do it. In my experience, in a wooded area of my own garden, it has proved to be one of the very few plants that can get the better of bluebells.* ❞

■ **CARE** A mulch of leaf mould or garden compost and an application of general fertilizer in spring for the first two or three years will help initial establishment.

■ **PROPAGATION** Layers will root naturally and pegging down, although not necessary, will encourage this. Take semi-ripe cuttings of juvenile shoots in late summer.

■ **PRUNING** None necessary, but may be cut back in spring if required. All-green shoots on variegated forms should be cut out.

■ **PROBLEMS** No serious problems, but leaf spots, aphids, red spider mites and scale insects occur occasionally.

SIZE Varies greatly (see Recommended varieties).
SITE AND SOIL Sun to full shade, but some variegated forms require some sun to maintain the variegation. Thrives in almost all soils and particularly useful for dry sites.
Weed Suppression Rating 5.
HARDINESS Most *Hedera helix* varieties are hardy, tolerating -15 to -20°C (5 to -4°F); *H. colchica* is moderately hardy, tolerating -10 to -15°C (14 to 5°F); *H. canariensis* is fairly hardy, tolerating -5 to -10°C (23 to 14°F).

■ **FEATURES** Evergreens with a wide variety of leaf forms, colours and textures. Growth habit varies, too, and there are ivies suitable for most situations.

Hedera helix 'Silver Queen'

SHRUBS

Helianthemum
Rock rose

The three closely related and mainly Mediterranean genera Helianthemum, Cistus *and* Halimium *all feature in this book, although they won't grow in all gardens; their requirements for light soil and sunny conditions mitigate against this.* Helianthemum *is probably the toughest of them. Where conditions are suitable, few low-growing plants offer more attractive flowers and serve as such delightful reminders of sunnier climes.*

■ **CARE** When planting in heavy soils, add some sharp grit to improve the drainage. Protect from cold winds.

■ **PROPAGATION** Take semi-ripe cuttings in summer. Species may be raised from seed sown in autumn.

■ **PRUNING** Trim back lightly after flowering to maintain a neat, compact habit.

■ **PROBLEMS** None.

■ **FEATURES** Low, spreading evergreens with small, often grey-green leaves. The main attraction is their succession of saucer-shaped summer flowers in a range of bright colours.

SIZE Most reach 20 x 30cm (8 x 12in), some are more vigorous at 30 x 45cm (12 x 18in). Short-lived shrubs, their eventual size achieved within 5 years.

SITE AND SOIL Full sun and shelter from cold winds essential. Any well-drained soil, particularly good on alkaline soils and other poor, dry sites.

Weed Suppression Rating 3–4.

HARDINESS Moderately hardy, tolerating -10 to -15°C (14 to 5°F).

Helianthemum 'Henfield Brilliant'

Hypericum
St John's Wort

One species of Hypericum *has achieved such success as a ground cover plant that its name is now almost synonymous with the concept – and with notoriety. If you really do want something impenetrable and almost ineradicable, this is it. If you don't, look elsewhere.*

■ **CARE** No special care necessary for the ground cover forms, which come as close as any shrubs to thriving on neglect.

■ **PROPAGATION** *Hypericum calycinum* produces suckers, and these may be removed from the parent plant for replanting, or the plant may be divided in autumn or spring. For all other forms, take semi-ripe cuttings in summer.

Recommended varieties

Helianthemum nummularium (common rock rose) variable plant with yellow, pink or white flowers, 50 x 60cm (20 x 24in). The following hybrids are among those most widely available: 'Amy Baring' AGM deep yellow flowers with orange centres; 'Ben Ledi' dark green foliage, bright deep rose-pink flowers; 'Boughton Double Primrose' dark green foliage, double primrose-yellow flowers; 'Cerise Queen' dark green foliage, double cerise-pink flowers; 'Fire Dragon' (syn. 'Mrs Clay') AGM orange-red flowers; 'Georgeham' pink and yellow flowers; 'Henfield Brilliant' AGM orange-red flowers; 'Jubilee' AGM green foliage, drooping, primrose-yellow double flowers; 'Mrs C.W. Earle' AGM dark green foliage, double scarlet flowers; 'Praecox' silver-grey foliage, lemon yellow flowers, early flowering; 'Raspberry Ripple' dark green foliage, white flowers with dark pink markings; 'Rhodanthe Carneum' (syn. 'Wisley Pink') AGM vigorous habit, silver-grey foliage, pale pink flowers; 'Rose of Leeswood' green foliage, double rose-pink flowers; 'The Bride' AGM silver-grey foliage, creamy white flowers; 'Wisley Primrose' AGM vigorous habit, pale primrose-yellow flowers.

■ **PRUNING** *H. calycinum* may be sheared back or a powered trimmer used to cut back the previous growth to ground level in early spring. Prune *H. x moserianum* in spring by removing any old, weak or thin shoots and then shortening the other stems back to their junction with strong shoots.

> **SIZE** Ground cover forms reach 30 x 75cm (12 x 30in) after 5 years; *H. calycinum* eventually spreads to 2m (6ft).
> **SITE AND SOIL** Full sun or partial shade, and in any garden soil. *H. calycinum* can tolerate deep shade and extreme soils such as very dry, acidic or alkaline, but will become a weed if planted inappropriately.
> **Weed Suppression Rating 5.**
> **HARDINESS** Forms recommended here are hardy, tolerating -15 to -20°C (5 to -4°F).

Hypericum calycinum

■ **PROBLEMS** Rust on *H. calycinum*.
■ **FEATURES** Grey-green to dark green foliage, some only evergreen in mild areas. The yellow, cup- or saucer-shaped flowers have prominent stamens.

> **Recommended varieties**
> *Hypericum calycinum* (rose of Sharon) evergreen with dark green foliage, yellow flowers from early summer to early autumn, an extremely robust plant, thriving even in dry shade, spreads extensively by creeping stolons; *H. x moserianum* AGM rounded, semi-evergreen shrub with dark green foliage, golden yellow flowers with red anthers from midsummer to autumn.

Leptospermum Tea tree

❝ Leptospermum *is another of those frustrating Australian genera that just aren't quite hardy enough to be dependable ingredients of gardens in cooler climates. The one I have chosen here has proved reliable in a fairly sheltered part of my own garden and I hope it may grace yours similarly.* ❞

■ **CARE** Apply an acidic mulch such as conifer needles in spring to prevent the soil from drying out.
■ **PROPAGATION** Sow seed of species in autumn, or take semi-ripe cuttings in summer.
■ **PRUNING** None necessary.
■ **PROBLEMS** None.
■ **FEATURES** Aromatic foliage, the

colour varying from silver-green to dark green depending on the species. Masses of small, usually white, pink or red flowers are borne from late spring to early summer, followed by woody seed capsules.

> **SIZE** Low-growing *L. rupestre* reaches 30 x 80cm (12 x 32in) after 5 years, ultimately 1 x 1.5m (3 x 5ft), but other species are more upright.
> **SITE AND SOIL** Warm, sunny site and acidic or neutral soil essential. Tolerant of alkaline or dry soils. Best suited to mild areas.
> **Weed Suppression Rating 2–3.**
> **HARDINESS** Most are barely hardy to fairly hardy, tolerating -5°C (23°F), but *L. rupestre* is moderately hardy, tolerating -10 to -15°C (14 to 5°F).

> **Recommended varieties**
> *L. rupestre* (syn. *L. humifusum*, *L. prostratum*) AGM dark green foliage, small white flowers, the hardiest species.

Leptospermum rupestre

Leucothoe

❝ This plant has been a big frustration to me. When first I grew it on a friend's recommendation many years ago, I didn't know enough about its site requirements and didn't bother to check. I was aware of the need for an acidic soil, but its essential need for moisture had eluded me. Don't be similarly unenlightened. ❞

■ **CARE** Mulch with an acidic material such as pine needles and apply general fertilizer in spring.
■ **PROPAGATION** Layer or take softwood cuttings in early summer.
■ **PRUNING** None necessary, but one-third of the shoots may be cut back to soil level each year to improve foliage quality.
■ **PROBLEMS** None.
■ **FEATURES** Deciduous or evergreen shrubs with narrow, leathery foliage, usually light green but red or purple tints can develop in winter. Small white flowers hang down from the stems in late spring or early summer.

SIZE Varies, but *L. walteri* reaches 60 x 60cm (24 x 24in) after 5 years, 2 x 3m (6 x 10ft) eventually.
SITE AND SOIL Better in light to moderate shade than full sun. Acidic, moist soil with plenty of humus.
Weed Suppression Rating 2–3.
HARDINESS Hardy, tolerating -15°C (5°F).

Recommended varieties
L. walteri (syn. *L. fontanesiana*) AGM evergreen, graceful arching stems, leathery green foliage with red tints in autumn and winter, white flowers in late spring, 'Rainbow' variegated leaves with irregular pink markings that age to creamy white, for the best leaf colour grow in light shade.

Lithodora

❝ There's a variety of Lithodora called 'Heavenly Blue' and it's a name that admirably sums up the qualities of these plants in general. For although there are forms in other colours, it's the delightful carpet of blue they create that for me is their enduring feature. ❞

■ **CARE** Give protection in the first winter after planting; leave undisturbed once established.
■ **PROPAGATION** Take semi-ripe cuttings in summer and keep them frost free over winter.
■ **PRUNING** None necessary.
■ **PROBLEMS** None.
■ **FEATURES** Low-growing evergreens with small, narrow leaves, often forming bristly mats. The main attraction is the mass of flowers that lasts all summer.

SIZE 30 x 50cm (12 x 20in) at maturity after 5 years.
SITE AND SOIL Sunny, sheltered position. All forms prefer well-drained soil but alkalinity tolerance varies.
Weed Suppression Rating 2.
HARDINESS Moderately hardy, tolerating -10 to -15°C (14 to 5°F)

Recommended varieties
Lithodora diffusa (syn. *Lithospermum diffusum, L. prostratum*) bright blue flowers in late spring to early summer, prefers moist but well-drained acidic soil, 'Alba' white flowers, 'Heavenly Blue' AGM trailing habit, azure flowers.

Leucothoe walteri 'Rainbow'

Lithodora diffusa 'Heavenly Blue'

Lonicera
Shrubby honeysuckle

❝ *I've spent many years trying to persuade people that there are shrubby honeysuckles and that the familiar tiny-leaved hedging plant that everyone knows but no one knows what to call is, in truth, one of them. It is quite unlike the familiar climbing honeysuckles but it is as good at covering the ground as they are at covering vertical supports.* ❞

■ **CARE** Apply general or rose fertilizer in spring.

■ **PROPAGATION** For *Lonicera pileata* take semi-ripe cuttings in summer and maintain in a cold frame.

■ **PRUNING** Many of the shrubby

Lonicera pileata

honeysuckles benefit from pruning to improve flower production but *L. pileata* is better left unpruned.

■ **PROBLEMS** None.

■ **FEATURES** Diverse genus of deciduous and evergreen shrubs and climbers. Some have attractive flowers, sometimes strongly scented, followed by usually black fruits. The ground cover form is evergreen or semi-evergreen and grown for its foliage and attractive twigs.

SIZE *L. pileata* reaches 1 x 1.5m (3 x 5ft) after 5 years, ultimately 1.5m (5ft) tall.

SITE AND SOIL Tolerates partial shade. Succeeds in most good garden soils.

Weed Suppression Rating 3–4.

HARDINESS Varies, but *L. pileata* is hardy, tolerating about -15°C (5°F)

Recommended varieties

Lonicera pileata evergreen to semi-evergreen, dwarf shrub with horizontal branches, dark green, shiny foliage, yellow-white flowers in later spring, translucent violet fruits.

Mahonia

❝ *Mahonias have yellow flowers, like so many other shrubs that flower in the early part of the year. They also have large evergreen leaves. Both of these attributes are widely appreciated. What is less readily realized is that when planted* en masse *they make rather dense and very effective ground cover.* ❞

■ **CARE** Mulch and apply rose fertilizer in spring.

■ **PROPAGATION** Suckering forms are most easily propagated by removing the suckers and transplanting them. Alternatively, take semi-ripe cuttings in late summer or hardwood cuttings in winter.

■ **PRUNING** None necessary, but pull out any unwanted suckers.

■ **PROBLEMS** None.

■ **FEATURES** Evergreen shrubs of various sizes, with dark green, spiny, architectural foliage and yellow flowers in winter or early spring. In most, the flowers are delightfully scented and followed by small, grape-like, blue or black fruits.

SIZE Ground cover forms reach 40cm x 1m (20in x 3ft) at maturity after 5 years.

SITE AND SOIL Native to the Americas, ground cover forms prefer drier soils and sunnier sites than many other mahonias. *M. nervosa* is intolerant of alkaline soils.

Weed Suppression Rating 2.

HARDINESS Hardy, tolerating about -15°C (5°F)

Recommended varieties

Mahonia aquifolium spiny, holly-like leaves, coarse suckering habit, bright yellow flowers in fairly small heads in spring, 'Apollo' larger, better flowers; *M. nervosa* large leathery leaves with red tints in winter, erect masses of small yellow flowers in late spring, blue-black fruits; *M. repens* leaves of medium size, yellow spring flowers on the end of the previous year's growth, black fruits, suckering habit.

SHRUBS

Muehlenbeckia

❝ *Tiny-leaved evergreens have a charm all of their own, and this rather vigorous, wiry shrub is one of the most charming. Its habit is dense enough for it to be used as a rather unusual subject for topiary, but the same characteristic works just as well in covering the soil. Bear in mind that it originates in fairly mild areas of the southern hemisphere and must be planted accordingly.* ❞

■ **CARE** Requires shelter from cold winds and is best given protection in the first winter after planting.
■ **PROPAGATION** Sow ripe seed in warmth in autumn. Layer plants, or take semi-ripe cuttings in summer and place in a warm propagator.
■ **PRUNING** None necessary, but may be cut back in spring to keep within bounds or clipped (may be used for topiary).
■ **PROBLEMS** None.
■ **FEATURES** Evergreen and deciduous twiggy shrubs or climbers. Clusters of scented green-yellow flowers in summer are followed by white fruits. Some plants bear flowers of only one sex, others of both.

SIZE Varies (see Recommended varieties).
SITE AND SOIL Sunny or lightly shaded site and moist but well-drained soil. Provide shelter from cold, drying winds.
Weed Suppression Rating 3–4.
HARDINESS Varies, but *M. complexa* is moderately hardy to hardy, tolerating at least -15°C (5°F) if sheltered from wind.

Recommended varieties
Muehlenbeckia complexa deciduous, although more or less evergreen in mild areas, plants vary in habit, some being dense shrubs with leathery leaves while others are climbers with long trails of softer leaves, shrubby forms reach about 1 x 1.5m (3 x 5ft) after 5 years and ultimately 2 x 2m (6 x 6ft), climbing or scrambling types 6 x 6m (20 x 20ft).

Muehlenbeckia complexa

Pachysandra

❝ *Rather like* Leucothoe *(see p. 34),* Pachysandra *at first disappointed me because although I knew it was shade tolerant, I didn't know that it is always a far more satisfactory plant in rich, moist soil. The places in my garden where I might use it are still too dry, but I know of other gardens where it romps away.* ❞

■ **CARE** Apply general fertilizer in spring, mulching until well established.
■ **PROPAGATION** Lift and divide plants in early spring or early autumn.
■ **PRUNING** None necessary.
■ **PROBLEMS** None.

SIZE 20 x 30–45cm (8 x 12–18in) at maturity after 5 years.
SITE AND SOIL Tolerates moderate to deep shade. Grows in most soils and tolerant of dry sites, but always best in deep, moist conditions. Avoid shallow, alkaline soils.
Weed Suppression Rating 4.
HARDINESS Very hardy, tolerating at least -20°C (-4°F).

Recommended varieties
Pachysandra terminalis AGM creeping rooting stems, white flowers in early spring, sometimes followed by white fruits, 'Green Carpet' more compact than the species, 10 x 20cm (4 x 8in), 'Variegata' AGM slower growing and rarely flowers but has attractive green leaves edged with cream.

FEATURES Evergreen sub-shrubs with dark green, toothed foliage. Small white flowers are borne in spring or summer.

Pachysandra terminalis

Photinia

❝Photinia *is a 'must have' genus for gardens with acidic soils, one of the essential components of the shrub border. It's less commonly thought of or used in a ground covering-role but it is easy to grow, undemanding and rather pretty – and you can't ask a great deal more than that.* ❞

■ **CARE** Mulch and apply general fertilizer in spring.
■ **PROPAGATION** Take semi-ripe cuttings in summer.

■ **PRUNING** None necessary for the ground cover forms. (Other photinias may be pruned to enhance the appeal of the spring foliage.)
■ **PROBLEMS** Fireblight although seldom as serious as on related shrubs.

> **SIZE** Most reach 1.5 x 2m (5 x 6ft) after 5 years, ultimately 4–6m (13–20ft) tall, but ground cover form recommended here is prostrate, reaching no more than 2m (6ft) after many years.
> **SITE AND SOIL** Thrives in light shade and most good garden soils, but best in humus-rich, moist sites.
> **Weed Suppression Rating 2.**
> **HARDINESS** Moderately hardy, tolerating -10 to -15°C (14 to 5°F).

■ **FEATURES** Deciduous and evergreen shrubs, usually upright and bushy but there are low-growing forms suitable as ground cover. The evergreens are most colourful in spring when the bright red young growths are evident; most seldom flower or fruit but *P. davidiana* is an exception. Deciduous photinias have good autumn colour, clusters of white flowers in spring and bright red fruits.

> **Recommended varieties**
> *Photinia davidiana* 'Prostrata' (syn. *Stranvaesia davidiana* 'Prostrata'), evergreen or semi-evergreen with older leaves turning red in autumn, white flowers in midsummer, bunches of bright red fruit.

Photinia davidiana **'Prostrata'**

Potentilla Cinquefoil

❝ *Whenever I'm asked to suggest the shrub with the longest flowering season,* Fuchsia *tops the list but* Potentilla *isn't far behind. This really is a most adaptable, amenable and versatile plant, very easy to grow and available now in a wide range of colours (some more attractive than others) and habits. While the tall varieties make imposing border plants, the low-growing types will provide a carpet at their feet.* ❞

■ **CARE** Mulch and apply rose fertilizer in spring.
■ **PROPAGATION** Take semi-ripe cuttings in summer, preferably with a 'heel' of old wood.
■ **PRUNING** None necessary, but old, twiggy growth may be removed after flowering and the rest of the shrub trimmed lightly. Shorten vigorous young shoots by one-half in spring for a more compact shape.
■ **PROBLEMS** None.
■ **FEATURES** Genus consisting of annuals, perennials and one shrub, *P. fruticosa* (shrubby cinquefoil). This is an attractive, deciduous plant with small green or grey-green leaves and a compact habit. The main feature lies in the flowers in yellow, orange, red, pink or white, although I find the reds very unsatisfactory. The flowers appear mainly in summer but also intermittently from late spring to the autumn.

SIZE *P. fruticosa* reaches 30–50 x 45cm (12–20 x 18in) after 5 years, its numerous cultivars varying from 75cm x 1m (30in x 3ft) for low-growing forms to 1.5 x 1.5m (5 x 5ft) for taller ones.
SITE AND SOIL Best in a sunny position, but worth trying in partial shade, not least because some flower colours (especially reds) tend to fade in bright sun. Any well-drained, fertile soil.
Weed Suppression Rating 2–3.
HARDINESS Hardy, tolerating -15 to -20°C (5 to -4°F)

Recommended varieties
Potentilla fruticosa 'Abbotswood' AGM low and spreading, white flowers, long flowering, 'Beesii' (syn. 'Argentea Nana') AGM dwarf, silver foliage, bright yellow flowers, 'Elizabeth' (syn. *P. arbuscula*) AGM round bush, 1 x 1.2m (3 x 4ft), rich yellow flowers, 'Manchu' (syn. 'Mandshurica') low and spreading, grey-green foliage, sparse white flowers but long flowering, 'Tangerine' AGM low and spreading, light copper-yellow flowers, best in partial shade, 'Tilford Cream' AGM dwarf, rich green foliage, creamy white flowers.

Potentilla fruticosa 'Manchu'

Prunus Cherry laurel

❝ *The cherry laurel is one of the foliage plants that has gained an unfortunate reputation, being associated in many gardeners' minds with the shrub garden of times past, part of that sombre greenery of the Victorian vicarage. You can, indeed, have too much of a green thing, but when interplanted with appropriately cheerful companions, this* Prunus *can play a very valuable role in the modern garden.* ❞

■ **CARE** Mulch and apply general fertilizer in spring.
■ **PROPAGATION** Take semi-ripe cuttings in late summer or hardwood cuttings in winter.
■ **PRUNING** None necessary, but may be clipped in midsummer and again in early autumn; use secateurs if possible, as shears cut through the large leaves, which then discolour.

Prunus laurocerasus 'Zabeliana'

■ **PROBLEMS** None, this species isn't prone to the many problems, such as silver-leaf, canker and aphids, that affect many other *Prunus*.

■ **FEATURES** Forms recommended here are all low, spreading evergreens with oval or narrow leaves. Clusters of small white flowers in spring are followed by black fruits in early autumn.

SIZE Ground cover forms reach 1 x 1–1.5m (3 x 3–5ft) after 5 years, eventual spread 1.5–2.5m (5–8ft).
SITE AND SOIL Full sun to deep shade, tolerant of water and honeydew dripping from overhanging trees. Most garden soils except thin and alkaline.
Weed Suppression Rating 5.
HARDINESS Very hardy, tolerating -20°C (-4°F).

Recommended varieties
Prunus laurocerasus 'Otto Luyken' AGM compact, spreading to 1m (3ft), then 1.5m (5ft), oval, shiny green leaves, 'Zabeliana' horizontal branches spreading to 1.5m (5ft), then 2.5m (8ft), willow-like leaves.

Pyracantha Firethorn

❝ *I've said elsewhere that good 'vertical' plants can be good 'horizontal' ones, too. Pyracantha is an instance of this, almost invariably being thought of as a wall shrub but equally valuable when it spreads sideways and forms a thorny, ground-covering barrier to intruders, both human and animal.* ❞

Pyracantha 'Soleil d'Or'

■ **CARE** Mulch and apply rose fertilizer in spring.
■ **PROPAGATION** Take semi-ripe cuttings in summer.
■ **PRUNING** None necessary when grown as ground cover.

SIZE *P.* 'Alexander Pendula' 50cm x 1.5m (20in x 5ft) after 5 years, ultimately 60cm (24in) tall, *P.* 'Soleil d'Or' 1 x 1m (3 x 3ft) after 5 years, ultimately spreads to 1.5m (5ft); there are many other, generally upright varieties unsuitable as ground cover.
SITE AND SOIL Sun or shade, particularly good for exposed or polluted areas. Most garden soils except thin and alkaline.
Weed Suppression Rating 1–2.
HARDINESS Very hardy, tolerating -20°C (-4°F).

■ **PROBLEMS** Aphids, fireblight, scab (which disfigures the fruits); birds readily feed on the fruits.
■ **FEATURES** Evergreens with rather viciously thorny branches and small, toothed leaves, which are sometimes variegated. White, hawthorn-like flowers appear in early summer. The main ornamental feature is the long-lasting red, orange or yellow fruits. Often grown as wall shrubs, the few semi-spreading varieties make tough and effective ground cover.

Recommended varieties
'Alexander Pendula' dense hummock with weeping branches, sparse fruits that start yellow and then turn red; 'Soleil d'Or' (syn. 'Golden Sun', 'Yellow Sun') deep golden yellow fruits, red stems, semi-spreading habit.

Rosa Ground cover roses

❝ There's been no doubt for a long time that ground cover roses exist; nurseries have been selling them for years. There's been no doubt, too, that many shrub roses have a spreading, cascading habit that also covers a considerable area of ground, even if they do so from some height. Recently, however, there has been something of a minor explosion in the range of specific ground cover varieties on offer and I continue to have mixed feelings about them. Some have attractive flowers, some are distinctly awful, but none of them really fulfils properly that desirable criterion of weed suppression. Grow them for their looks, not their function ❞

Rosa 'Max Graf'

■ **CARE** Ensure that the ground is thoroughly prepared, digging in well-rotted organic matter and removing all perennial weeds before planting. Apply rose fertilizer in spring, then top up with a deep (10–15cm/4–6in) mulch. Feed again after the first flowers have faded in early summer. Dead-head faded flowers if practical.

■ **PROPAGATION** Take hardwood cuttings in autumn. Ramblers with flexible stems can also be layered.

■ **PRUNING** Very little necessary, but cut out any dead or diseased stems. Ramblers with long, flexible stems may be kept under control by light pruning after flowering. Pull out any unwanted suckers.

■ **PROBLEMS** Aphids; most roses are susceptible to a greater or lesser

SIZE Most reach 60cm–1m x 1.2–2m (2–3ft x 4–6ft) at maturity after 5 years, although spread may vary.

SITE AND SOIL Full sun for best flower production, although very light shade helps to prevent some varieties fading; sheltered site preferred as flowers will be damaged less by wind and rain. Rich clay or loam soil ideal, but most garden soils are suitable if plenty of well-rotted organic matter is added annually; thin, alkaline soils rarely give good results. New roses often fail if planted in soil that previously contained roses, so either plant in a clean site or replace the soil with fresh in each planting position.

Weed Suppression Rating 1–2.

HARDINESS Very hardy, tolerating at least -20°C (-4°F).

Recommended varieties

Note synonyms have not been given here as some varieties have many that are seldom used; the names given are those likely to be used by most nurseries and garden centres: 'Avon' pale pink buds open to semi-double pearl-white flowers, continuous flowering; 'Ferdy' double bright pink flowers, continuous flowering; 'Macrantha Raubritter' semi-double silver-pink flowers, some scent; 'Max Graf' rose-pink flowers with golden centres, some scent; *Rosa nitida*, dwarf suckering species, rose-red flowers, scarlet hips, foliage has autumn colour; 'Norfolk' double yellow flowers, repeat flowering; 'Nozomi' AGM silver-pink flowers fading to white; 'Paulii' white flowers with yellow stamens, very thorny, vigorous stems 3–4m (10–13ft) long; 'Pink Bells' double bright pink flowers, tolerates light shade; 'Pink Flower Carpet' AGM double bright pink flowers, continuous flowering, long-lasting foliage, one of the biggest selling roses of recent years and aggressively marketed but a hideous colour; *R. x polliniana* rose-pink buds open to blush flowers with yellow anthers, rambling habit that spreads to 3m (10ft); 'Red Blanket' AGM semi-double, rose-red flowers fading to white at petal bases; 'Rosy Cushion' AGM semi-double pink flowers with white centres, some scent, tolerates light shade; 'Snow Carpet' AGM prostrate habit, double white flowers, some scent, repeat flowering, only 15 x 45cm (6 x 18in); 'Suffolk' scarlet flowers with gold stamens, repeat flowering, orange-red hips, only 45cm x 1m (18in x 3ft), tolerates light shade; 'Sunshine' semi-double yellow flowers, spreading habit, continuous flowering, the latest offering from the nursery that brought you one of the most vulgar plants of recent years in 'Pink Flower Carpet'; 'Surrey' double pink flowers, tolerates light shade; 'Sussex' double buff-apricot flowers, repeat flowering; 'Swany' AGM double white flowers, continuous flowering, sprawling shoots; 'White Flower Carpet' white version of 'Pink Flower Carpet'; *R. wichurana* parent of many ramblers, semi-evergreen, scented white flowers with yellow stamens in late summer, tiny red hips, trailing stems that root as they grow, 2 x 6m (6 x 20ft).

extent to three diseases – powdery mildew, blackspot and rust – although some varieties have some resistance.

■ **FEATURES** Deciduous, thorny shrubs of varying habits, including spreading ground cover forms. The flowers are the main attraction, appearing in one flush in early summer, or repeating or continuous from summer until autumn.

Rosa 'Nozomi'

Rosa 'Pink Flower Carpet'

SHRUBS

Rhododendron

❝ *Most of the ground covering that rhododendrons do is over large areas of countryside from which many people would rather see them removed. I cannot argue against the fact that* Rhododendron ponticum *has in some places become a woody weed – but that simply serves to emphasize that scaled-down versions, smaller species usually with large, evergreen leaves sweeping down to ground level, do have the ability to cloak small areas, too.* ❞

■ **CARE** Plant so that the rootball is covered by no more than about 3cm (1¼in) of soil. Mulch with an acidic material such as conifer needles and apply rose fertilizer in spring. Pull off

dead flowerheads using finger and thumb whenever the plant is of manageable size, but be careful not to remove the buds that will give rise to next year's flowers.
■ **PROPAGATION** Difficult from hardwood cuttings, taken in late autumn to winter, but many forms can be layered.
■ **PRUNING** None necessary.
■ **PROBLEMS** Leaf spot, powdery mildew, bud blast, vine weevil.
■ **FEATURES** Most are evergreens, with medium to large, glossy green leaves, some with a felt-like layer (called an indumentum) on the undersides. A few are semi-evergreen or deciduous, the latter including some azaleas with good autumn colour. Large clusters of beautiful flowers, in a wide range of sizes and in colours ranging from red, pink and lilac to orange, yellow and white, are produced in spring.

Rhododendron yakushimanum

SIZE Varies greatly, but low-growing species and hardy hybrids that are most useful for ground cover reach 1–3 x 1–2m (3–10 x 3–6ft) ultimately, although this is achieved slowly.
SITE AND SOIL Light to moderate shade preferred to prevent frost or wind damage to flowers and young foliage but some forms, especially azaleas, tolerate sun. Acidic soil, enriched with humus so that it is moist but not waterlogged. Intolerant of any alkalinity or dryness.
Weed Suppression Rating 4.
HARDINESS Fairly hardy to very hardy; most are moderately hardy, tolerating -10 to -15°C (14 to 5°F).

Recommended varieties
There are numerous varieties, most of which in massed planting make good, large ground cover, but on a smaller scale the following species and its many hybrids are particularly effective: *Rhododendron yakushimanum* (syn. *R. degronianum* subsp. *yakushimanum*) narrow dark green foliage with red-brown indumentum, rose-pink buds opening to pink flowers that fade to white, very hardy, suitable for sun or shade, small dome-shaped species up to 1 x 1.2m (3 x 4ft). Evergreen azaleas (Japanese azaleas) can withstand hotter, drier sites than dwarf rhododendrons; plant in full sun in cool areas, light shade in warmer districts.

Ribes

❝ Ribes *offers another example of a genus of which we have one general perception but within which there is the odd species with very different attributes.* Ribes laurifolium *(laurel-leaved currant) is as far removed as can be imagined from its relatives the currants, both flowering and fruiting, but in the context of this book it's certainly none the worse for that.* ❞

■ **CARE** Mulch and apply rose fertilizer in spring.
■ **PROPAGATION** Take semi-ripe cuttings in autumn.

■ **PROBLEMS** None.

■ **FEATURES** Most species are decid-uous, tall, spring-flowering shrubs but *Ribes laurifolium* is a dwarf evergreen with winter flowers.

SIZE 50 x 50cm (20 x 20in) after 5 years, 1 x 1.5m (3 x 5ft) ultimately.
SITE AND SOIL Tolerant of most sites and soils.
Weed Suppression Rating 4.
HARDINESS Hardy, tolerating -15 to -20°C (5 to -4°F).

Recommended varieties
Ribes laurifolium evergreen, leathery, dark green leaves, green-yellow flowers in late winter to early spring, female plants have red fruits that age to black.

Ribes laurifolium

Rosmarinus Rosemary

❝*For many people, rosemary is used to cover little more than the joint of roast lamb. Yet, like* Buxus *(see p. 18), among others, it's yet another instance of a plant that is dense enough to make a good hedge and, in the guise of different vari-eties, makes a good ground cover plant, too. I happen to think that it has very pretty flowers also.* ❞

■ **CARE** Mulch and apply general or rose fertilizer in spring.
■ **PROPAGATION** Take semi-ripe cuttings in summer.
■ **PRUNING** Cut out the oldest one-third of the shoots in spring to rejuv-enate old and woody plants.
■ **PROBLEMS** None.
■ **FEATURES** Aromatic evergreens with needle-like, blue-green foliage, widely used as a herb. Small clusters of flowers, usually blue or mauve, some-times pink or white, appear from mid-spring to early summer.

SIZE Varies greatly, but ground cover form recommended here reaches about 15 x 60cm (6 x 24in) after 5 years.
SITE AND SOIL Full sun and well-drained soil, but tolerates light shade. Avoid waterlogged and extremely acidic or alkaline soils.
Weed Suppression Rating 1-2
HARDINESS Ground cover forms are among the less hardy varieties, most being fairly hardy to moder-ately hardy, tolerating -5 to -15°C (23 to -5°F).

Recommended varieties
Rosmarinus officinalis (common rose-mary) has a number of varieties, but the best for ground cover is Prostratus Group (syn. *R. corsicus* 'Prostratus', *R.* x *lavandulaceus*, *R. officinalis* var. *lavandulaceus*, *R. o.* var. *repens*, *R. repens*) AGM prostrate, light blue flowers in early summer.

Rosmarinus officinalis **Prostratus Group**

SHRUBS

Rubus Ornamental bramble

❝ *You need only try picking wild blackberries to discover how impenetrable a thicket the bramble can make. Those long, arching stolons root where they land, and only the most adventurous rabbit is likely to make any headway underneath. Their ornamental relatives aren't quite so aggressively vigorous but are nevertheless effective enough to be used alongside motorways and in similar large, barren places.* ❞

■ **CARE** Mulch and apply general fertilizer in spring.

■ **PROPAGATION** The long, trailing stems root readily where they touch the ground.

■ **PRUNING** If *Rubus tricolor* is grown in the wilder parts of a garden it may be left unpruned, otherwise cut back to the crown each spring to encourage new foliage; this may be done with a powered trimmer. *R. pentalobus* requires no pruning.

■ **PROBLEMS**
None.

■ **FEATURES**
Evergreen or deciduous shrubs or climbers with attractive white summer flowers, foliage, stems or edible red fruits, depending on the species. Stems are covered in prickles.

> **SIZE** Varies greatly; alpine *R. pentalobus* is only 5 x 20cm (2 x 8in) after 5 years, ultimate spread 60cm (24in), whereas *R. tricolor* reaches 60cm x 3m (24in x 10ft) after 5 years, with more or less indefinite ultimate spread.
> **SITE AND SOIL** Full sun to full shade. Most garden soils except waterlogged.
> **Weed Suppression Rating 4–5.**
> **HARDINESS** Very hardy, tolerating at least -20°C (-4°F), but foliage may be browned by very cold winds.

> **Recommended varieties**
> *Rubus pentalobus* (syn. *R. calycinoides*) evergreen, prostrate shrub with a mat of glossy green, wrinkled leaves with grey undersides, white flowers in early summer but often hidden by the foliage, red fruits may follow; *R. tricolor* evergreen, carpeting scrambler with long trailing stems covered with red bristles, heart-shaped dark green leaves with white undersides, white flowers in mid-summer, edible red fruits may follow.

Rubus tricolor

Salix Willow

❝ *Everyone knows that the willow is without peer as a plant for streamsides and wet soil plantings, but rather few would give it high priority as ground cover. Nonetheless, some of the closest, tightest-growing, most prostrate ground cover in my garden is a knotted mat of* Salix repens *at the edge of my gravel garden. These low-growing, dwarf, mainly alpine* Salix species *are something rather special.* ❞

■ **CARE** No special care necessary.

■ **PROPAGATION** Take semi-ripe cuttings in summer or hardwood cuttings in late autumn or winter; these root very readily, but named varieties must be grafted.

■ **PRUNING** None necessary for dwarf forms.

■ **PROBLEMS** Aphids, caterpillars, beetles, honey fungus.

■ **FEATURES** Large and diverse genus of trees and shrubs, mostly deciduous. Varied features of interest include buds, catkins, winter stem colour and summer foliage.

> **SIZE** Varies greatly (see Recommended varieties).
> **SITE AND SOIL** Best in full sun. Most soils except thin and alkaline, especially good on wet, heavy soils although alpine forms require free drainage.
> **Weed Suppression Rating 4.**
> **HARDINESS** Very hardy, tolerating -20°C or below (-4°F or below).

Recommended varieties

Salix alpina (syn. *S.* 'Jacquinii') low, spreading shrub, glossy round leaves, males have purple catkins that turn yellow, females have green catkins, 25 x 20cm (10 x 8in); *S. x cottetii* vigorous, low, spreading shrub, long trailing stems form a carpet several metres (yards) across, glossy dark green leaves with pale undersides, catkins in early spring before the leaves, 25 x 50cm (10 x 20in); *S. x finnmarchica* low, spreading shrub, small leaves, catkins in early spring before the leaves, 30 x 50cm (12 x 20in); *S. x grahamii* low, spreading shrub, glossy green leaves, erect catkins form after the leaves, 30 x 50cm (12 x 20in); *S. repens* (creeping willow) species and its varieties are very variable in size and from, ranging from creeping plants, 10 x 60cm (4 x 24in), to more upright plants, 60cm x 1.5m (24in x 5ft), grey-green leaves silver-white beneath, grey male catkins before the leaves, *S. r.* var. *argentea* AGM semi-prostrate with silver leaves, small but numerous silver catkins, 'Voorthuizen' slender prostrate stems, small silver leaves, tiny catkins; *S. uva-ursi* (bearberry willow) low, spreading shrub, small glossy green leaves, catkins appear with the leaves in spring, 30 x 60cm (12 x 24in).

Santolina Cotton lavender

❝ *In the days before dwarf box (see p. 18) became popular for edging formal gardens, cotton lavender was used instead. Its compact, rather dense growth still makes it a good covering plant.* ❞

- **CARE** No special care necessary, as long as the lack of hardiness is taken into account.
- **PROPAGATION** Take semi-ripe cuttings in summer (these root most readily with bottom heat).
- **PRUNING** Cut back by at least one-half every spring to maintain a bushy, neat habit. Trim lightly after flowering.
- **PROBLEMS** None.

- **FEATURES** Small evergreen shrubs grown for their mounds of aromatic foliage. Button-like flowers of yellow or white appear in summer.

SIZE Most, including *S. pinnata*, reach 60cm x 1m (24in x 3ft) after 5 years; plants are best replaced after several years.
SITE AND SOIL Full sun and well-drained soil.
Weed Suppression Rating 2.
HARDINESS Barely hardy to fairly hardy, tolerating 0 to -10°C (32 to 14°F).

Recommended varieties
Santolina pinnata (syn. *S. tomentosa*) rounded bush, smooth, divided, mid-green leaves, white flowers in mid- to late summer.

Santolina pinnata

Salix repens

SHRUBS

Sarcococca Christmas box

❝ *No, not a seasonal gift – Christmas box is a member of the box family that flowers in winter. Like many winter flowers, they are individually small but beautifully fragrant: winter insects need an extra incentive. But it is the dense, evergreen foliage that finds the plant an entry here. It's a relatively uncommon species and worth growing for whatever reason.* ❞

■ **CARE** No special care necessary.
■ **PROPAGATION** Transplant rooted suckers or take hardwood cuttings in autumn.
■ **PRUNING** None necessary.
■ **PROBLEMS** If it becomes invasive, dig up suckers after severing them from the parent plant with a spade.
■ **FEATURES** Small evergreen shrubs offering attractive foliage, winter flowers and fruits. They have narrow, dark green leaves and clusters of tiny white flowers with a heady scent, followed by the fruits.

SIZE Most reach 60cm–1m x 60cm –1m (24–3ft x 24–3ft) after 5 years; ultimately taller forms reach 1.2–1.5m (4-5ft) tall, but ground cover form recommended here tends to remain low.
SITE AND SOIL Ideal for shade, although tolerates full sun if soil is moist. Moist but well-drained loam preferred.
Weed Suppression Rating 3.
HARDINESS Hardy, tolerating -15 to -20°C (5 to -4°F)

Recommended varieties
Sarcococca hookeriana var. *humulis*, a ground cover form of the more widely grown *S. h.* var. *digyna*, remains at 60 x 60cm (24 x 24in); *S. ruscifolia* pointed dark green leaves, creamy white flowers from late winter to early spring, red fruits in summer, 75 x 75cm (30 x30in) after 5 years, ultimately 1.2m (4ft) tall.

Stephanandra

❝ *It would have to be called 'Stephanandra', is the general comment when I warmly recommend this plant. But I would recommend it whatever its name, because this is certainly in my top five ground cover plants – and in my top three deciduous forms. I have recently planted a new area in which a collection of fastigiate trees grows from a billowing carpet of this lovely low-growing shrub. In ten years, it will be stunning.* ❞

■ **CARE** Apply general fertilizer in spring.

SIZE Most reach 1 x 2m (3 x 6ft) after 5 years, ultimately 1.5–2.5m (5–8ft) tall, but ground cover form recommended here is a low-growing domed mat, ultimately about 60cm x 2m (24in x 6ft).
SITE AND SOIL Most.
Weed Suppression Rating 4.
HARDINESS Very hardy, tolerating -20°C (-4°F) or below.

Sarcococca hookeriana var. humulis

■ **PROPAGATION** Layer, or remove naturally rooted layers. Take semi-ripe cuttings in summer.

■ **PRUNING** None necessary; alternatively, a proportion of the oldest wood may be cut out each spring to prevent congestion.

■ **PROBLEMS** None.

■ **FEATURES** Deciduous shrubs with a graceful but dense spreading habit, attractively shaped hawthorn-like foliage with good autumn colour, red-orange stems and tiny green-white flowers in summer.

Recommended varieties
Stephanandra incisa 'Crispa' (syn. *S. 'Prostrata'*) mound-like habit, small hawthorn-like leaves.

Stephanandra incisa 'Crispa'

Symphoricarpos Snowberry

" The snowberry isn't a plant with particular winter features. It derives its name from the globular fruits, which in the most familiar form are snow-white. They stand out against rather sparse foliage, but the ground cover benefit comes from the closely packed mass of twigs. "

■ **CARE** No special care necessary, but benefits from a mulch and rose fertilizer applied in spring.

■ **PROPAGATION** Transplant naturally rooted suckers. Take semi-ripe cuttings in summer or hardwood cuttings in winter.

■ **PRUNING** Prune to 30cm (12in) high after planting to encourage dense cover; no further pruning necessary.

■ **PROBLEMS** None, apart from unwanted suckering.

■ **FEATURES** Deciduous shrubs with dense, twiggy growth and a suckering habit. Grown mainly for their large, spherical, long-lasting pink, white or red fruits, the flowers are insignificant but popular with bees. Useful plants for difficult conditions.

SIZE Most reach 1.2 x 1.2m (4 x 4ft) after 5 years, ultimately 1.5–2m (5–6ft) tall, but ground cover form recommended here reaches 60cm x 1.5m (2 x 5ft) after 5 years, ultimately only 1m (3ft) tall.
SITE AND SOIL Thrives in sun, but especially useful as tolerates deep shade and almost any soil, including dry or neglected sites.
Weed Suppression Rating 2–3.
HARDINESS Very hardy, tolerating -20°C (-4°F) or below.

Symphoricarpos x chenaultii 'Hancock'

Recommended varieties
Symphoricarpos x chenaultii 'Hancock' dense, sprawling shrub, leaves are bronze when young then bright green, lilac-pink fruits in autumn.

Vaccinium

" Think of kilometre after kilometre of wild, upland moor covered with bilberry bushes and you will realize just how effective such individually unspectacular plants can be. If you have a small garden, however, they will be lost. "

■ **CARE** Mulch with conifer needles, sawdust or other acidic material in spring.

■ **PROPAGATION** Take softwood cuttings in late summer and provide bottom heat. Species may be raised from seed sown in autumn, and low-growing forms can be layered.

■ **PRUNING** None necessary, but plants may be trimmed in spring to keep them tidy.

■ **PROBLEMS** None, but plants may be damaged by rabbits or deer in wilder gardens.

■ **FEATURES** Large genus of deciduous and evergreen shrubs for acidic soils. Autumn colour from leaves or fruits is the main attraction, but some have small, attractive flowers in late spring or early summer.

SIZE Varies, most remaining under 1m (3ft) for first 5 years but spread may be 1m (3ft) or indefinite (see Recommended varieties).
SITE AND SOIL Full sun or partial shade. Moist, acidic soil essential.
Weed Suppression Rating 3.
HARDINESS Varies from barely hardy, tolerating 0 to -5°C (32 to 23°F) to very hardy, tolerating at least -20°C (-4°F).

Recommended varieties
Vaccinium delavayi compact evergreen, dark green leaves, white flowers with a pink flush, edible red-purple fruits, 20 x 20cm (8 x 8in) after 5 years, ultimately 1–1.5m (3–5ft) tall, hardy, tolerating about -15°C (5°F); *V. glaucoalbum* AGM compact evergreen with suckering habit, stiff oval dark green leaves with white undersides, white to pale pink flowers, edible black fruits with blue-white bloom in autumn, 1 x 1m (3 x 3ft) after 5 years, ultimately 1.2m (4ft) tall, fairly hardy, tolerating about -10°C (14°F); *V. moupinense* compact evergreen, leathery dark green leaves, dark red-brown flowers, edible purple-black fruits, 60 x 90cm (24 x 36in), fairly hardy, tolerating about -10°C (14°F); *V. myrtillus* (bilberry) vigorous, creeping deciduous shrub, bright green leaves often red in autumn, pink flowers in late spring and early summer, edible blue-black fruits, may be invasive, 30cm (12in) x indefinite, very hardy; *V. vitis-idaea* (cowberry) creeping evergreen with underground rhizomes, small dark green foliage with red tints, white to pink flowers, edible but acidic bright red fruits, 25cm (10in) x indefinite, very hardy.

Vaccinium moupinense

Viburnum

" One of the biggest, most important but relatively unglamorous of shrub genera might be expected to have some lower growing species and varieties – and so it is. Although only a handful of the more than 150 total species are really low and dense, I should add that many of the taller growing types will be pretty effective, too, where space permits. "

■ **CARE** Mulch and apply general fertilizer in spring. Plant one male *Viburnum davidii* to every five females for reliable fruit production.

■ **PROPAGATION** Take semi-ripe cuttings in summer or autumn. Sow seed in autumn and leave in a cold frame over winter.

■ **PRUNING** None necessary.

■ **PROBLEMS** None.

■ **FEATURES** Large genus of deciduous and evergreen shrubs offering a variety of foliage, flower and fruit features. The best ground cover form is *V. davidii*, a low-growing, densely branched evergreen with bold foliage and metallic-blue fruit for which both male and female plants are necessary.

Viburnum davidii

SIZE Varies greatly, but *V. davidii* reaches 1 x 1m (3 x 3ft) after 5 years, 1.5 x 1.5m (5 x 5ft) ultimately.
SITE AND SOIL Sun or moderate shade and tolerant of windy sites. Any garden soil except very wet or very dry.
Weed Suppression Rating 4.
HARDINESS Hardy, tolerating -15 to -20°C (5 to -4°F)

Recommended varieties
Viburnum davidii AGM large, oval, leathery dark green foliage, small dull white flowers in early summer, turquoise-blue fruits on female plants (if a male plant is present) from late summer to early winter.

Vinca Periwinkle

6 6 *The pre-eminence of the periwinkles as ground cover plants has been slightly dented in recent years by the increasingly common rust disease that causes havoc on* Vinca major. *If it is a problem in your area, restrict yourself to the lower-growing, more restrained but much prettier* V. minor. 9 9

■ **CARE** Mulch only until well established. Apply general fertilizer in spring.
■ **PROPAGATION** Remove naturally rooted layers, or take semi-ripe cuttings in early summer or hardwood cuttings in winter.
■ **PRUNING** None necessary, but to keep plants within bounds they may be cut back hard in spring with shears or a powered trimmer.
■ **PROBLEMS** Rust on *Vinca major*.
■ **FEATURES** Evergreens with a fairly vigorous trailing habit and small to medium oval-shaped foliage that is often attractively variegated. Small tubular flowers, usually blue, appear in early summer, then intermittently until autumn.

SIZE *V. major* is 45cm (18in) tall, *V. minor* 20cm (8in) tall, both with more or less indefinite spread.
SITE AND SOIL Full sun to deep shade, but some sun necessary for best flower production. Most soils except very dry.
Weed Suppression Rating 5.
HARDINESS *V. major*, *V. minor* and varieties of both are very hardy, tolerating at least -20°C (-4°F).

Vinca minor 'Aureovariegata'

Recommended varieties
Vinca major medium-sized, oval plain green foliage, bright blue flowers, 'Maculata' (syn. 'Aureomaculata') dark yellow-green with lighter margins, pale blue flowers, 'Variegata' AGM light green foliage with pale yellow margins, blue-mauve flowers; *V. minor* small oval, plain green foliage, blue-pink or purple flowers, f. *alba* white flowers, 'Alba Variegata' yellow leaf variegation, white flowers, 'Argenteovariegata' AGM dull green foliage with pale yellow margins and midribs, violet-blue flowers, 'Atropurpurea' AGM green foliage striped and edged with yellow, blue flowers, 'Aureovariegata' green leaves striped and edged with yellow, blue flowers, 'Azurea Flore Pleno' AGM dark green foliage, double, red-purple flowers, 'Gertrude Jekyll' AGM green leaves, creamy white flowers, 'Multiplex' double purple flowers, 'Silver Service' grey-green leaves with silver variegation, double mid-blue flowers.

CONIFERS

Juniperus Juniper

❝ *Junipers have long been* the *ground-covering conifers, the old 'Pfitzeriana' types concealing more drain and manhole covers than I care to imagine. These older types have now been supplemented and in some measure replaced by more manageable, lower-growing but scarcely less effective varieties.* ❞

■ **CARE** Mulch and apply general fertilizer in spring.

■ **PROPAGATION** Take semi-ripe cuttings in summer or hardwood cuttings in winter, although rooting is often difficult without misting. Ripe seed may be sown in pots in autumn and left in a cold frame, but germination

Juniperus communis 'Hornibrookii'

is erratic and can take several years.

■ **PRUNING** None necessary; may be trimmed lightly if required but will not regenerate from old wood.

■ **PROBLEMS** Aphids, phytophthora.

■ **FEATURES** Evergreen conifers with sharp, needle-like foliage that ages to fleshy scales. Foliage may be green, yel-

Recommended varieties

There are numerous varieties of low-growing juniper, and forms listed here are those of which I have some personal knowledge; the newer forms may not all have been grown for long enough for their full potential to be known, so be aware that they may spread further than indicated: *Juniperus communis* var. *depressa* (Canadian juniper) prostrate with up-turned shoots, dwarf but wide spreading, yellow-green foliage that turns bronze in winter, 60cm x 1.5m (2 x 5ft), 'Depressa Aurea' spreading habit with semi-erect branches, golden yellow foliage in spring, bronze to green over winter, 60cm x 1.5m (2 x 5ft), 'Effusa' wide spreading, semi-prostrate, green foliage with silver-white undersides, 60cm x 1.5m

(2 x 5ft), 'Hornibrookii' creeping dwarf form that takes on the shape of the object it covers, small sharp foliage, silver-white beneath, 40cm x 1.5m (16in x 5ft), 'Repanda' AGM dwarf creeping habit, grey-green foliage with bronze tints in winter, 30cm x 2m (1 x 6ft) after 10 years; *J. conferta* (shore juniper) dense, creeping branches, apple-green foliage, male and female flowers on one plant, purple-black fruits, 30cm x 1m (1 x 3ft) after 5 years, then spreads by 10cm (4in) a year; *J. horizontalis* (creeping juniper) long branches, blue-grey foliage with sharp points, dark blue fruit, 30cm (12in) x indefinite, 'Bar Harbor' scale-like foliage, blue-green but turns purple in winter, 30cm x 1.5–2m (12in x 5–6ft), eventually spreads to 5m (16ft) or more, 'Blue Chip' (syn. 'Blue Moon') distinctive

bright blue foliage, retains the same colour all year round, carpet habit, eventually 50cm x 3m (20in x 10ft), 'Emerald Spreader' mat-like, flat shrub, bright green foliage, eventually 30cm x 3m (1 x 10ft), Glauca Group dense blue carpet, 30cm (12in) tall with trailing fringes to 3m (10ft), 'Prince of Wales' slow-growing mat, bright green foliage with blue tints, purple flushed in winter, 15cm x 1–1.2m (6in x 3–4ft) after 5 years, then spreads by 10–15cm (4–6in) per year, 'Wiltonii' (syn. 'Blue Rug') AGM long ground-hugging branches, one of the bluest, 30cm x 3m (1 x 10ft) after 10 years; *J. x pfitzeriana* 'Blound' (syn. 'Gold Sovereign', *J. x media* 'Blound') arching, spreading habit, yellow foliage, 1.2 x 3.5m (4 x 11ft), 'Gold Coast' low, spreading habit, yellow foliage, 60–90cm x 1.5–2m (24–36in x

ow, grey or almost blue. Tiny flowers
re borne at the shoot tips, and small
lue or black cones (which resemble
ruits) occur if male and female plants
re present, although not on *Juniperus
horizontalis* and its varieties.

SIZE Varies greatly, even among
ground cover forms, but most are
under 1m (3ft) tall with a spread of
1.5-2m (5-6ft) after 5 years. Some
spread more or less indefinitely,
growing 10cm (4in) or so each year.
SITE AND SOIL Full sun to light
shade, with shelter from cold winds.
Most well-drained garden soils,
including dry and alkaline.
Weed Suppression Rating 4.
HARDINESS Most are very hardy,
tolerating -20°C (-4°F) or below.

5–6ft), 'Old Gold' AGM slower grow-
ng than many other varieties, dense
semi-prostrate habit, bronze-gold
foliage, fades slightly in winter, 1–1.2 x
1.2–2m (3–4 x 4–6ft), 'Pfitzeriana'
AGM long arching branches, scale-like
green foliage with blue tints, eventually 3 x 5m (10 x 16ft); *J. sabina*
'Tamariscifolia' (savin) flat-topped
shape with horizontal, overlapping
branches, dark green foliage with an
unpleasant smell when crushed, tips
die back after hard frosts, ideally
grown between rocks, at the edge of
raised beds or on sandy banks, 20
30cm (8 x 12in) after 10 years, eventually 1 x 1.2m (3 x 4ft); *J. squamata*
'Blue Carpet' AGM slow growing,
ow, arching, blue-grey foliage, sharp
pointed needles, 30cm x 1.2–1.5m
(1 x 4–5ft).

Juniperus squamata **'Blue Carpet'**

CONIFERS

Picea Spruce

❝ *While there are a good many varieties of low-growing spruce (most notably the so-called 'blue spruces'), most are of too open a texture to be of real value for any proper ground-covering purpose. I have selected two that are, however, rather effective in this role.* ❞

■ **CARE** Plant in spring, mulch young trees and feed with general fertilizer in spring.

■ **PROPAGATION** Difficult to propagate without a misting facility.

Picea abies 'Repens'

■ **PRUNING** None necessary, except to remove any upright branches on prostrate plants. They do not regenerate from old wood and pruning can spoil the shape; any removal of damaged branches should be done in winter.

■ **PROBLEMS** Aphids, red spider mite, adelgids, diebacks, root rots.

■ **FEATURES** Evergreen conifers, appearing superficially like firs but the needles are borne on short, woody pegs that remain after the leaves have fallen. Insignificant 'flowers' are borne in late winter to spring. The green cones age to brown, although dwarf forms do not usually produce them.

SIZE Varies (see Recommended varieties).

SITE AND SOIL Open site essential, intolerant of shade. Most garden soils except very poor, dry or alkaline (although some varieties tolerate alkaline soils). Not for coastal areas.

Weed Suppression Rating 3.

HARDINESS Most are hardy, tolerating about -15°C (5°F), but late spring frost can damage new growth and young trees.

Recommended varieties
Picea abies 'Repens' (Norway spruce) prostrate, slow-growing flat-topped bush with branches in layers, 30–40 cm x 1–1.5m (12–16in x 3–5ft); *P. pungens* 'Glauca Prostrata' (syn. 'Prostrata') spreading, ground-creeping branches, blue needles, very hardy, 25cm x 1.5m (10in x 5ft) after 20 years.

Podocarpus

❝ *Podocarps aren't common garden plants at the best of times. They are conifers, but are more closely related to yews than to the pines and spruces. The main reason they aren't more widely grown is that most aren't really sufficiently hardy although the New Zealand species I recommend here is a spreading alpine and has proved tough enough in my own garden.* ❞

■ **CARE** Give protection over the first winter after planting, then mulch and apply general fertilizer in spring.

■ **PROPAGATION** Take semi-ripe cuttings in early autumn and root them over winter, providing some bottom heat.

■ **PRUNING** None necessary, but may be lightly sheared into shape in summer.

■ **PROBLEMS** Scale insects.

■ **FEATURES** Evergreen conifers with stiff, leathery, yew-like foliage. Male plants bear catkin-like flowers in late spring to early summer, female plants

SIZE *P. nivalis* reaches 60 x 80cm (24 x 32in) after 5 years, ultimately 1–2 x 2–3m (3–6 x 6–10ft).

SITE AND SOIL Open site essential. Most well-drained garden soils; thrives in alkaline conditions.

Weed Suppression Rating 3.

HARDINESS Most are from the southern hemisphere and really successful only in mild areas, but a few like *P. nivalis* are hardy, tolerating -15 to -20°C (5 to -4°F).

have small cones. If male and female plants are grown together, the females may produce fleshy red fruits.

Recommended varieties
Podocarpus nivalis (alpine totara) low, spreading mound, dense branches, small, narrow olive-green foliage, which turns bronze or purple in winter, fruits readily.

Podocarpus nivalis

Taxus Yew

❝ ❝*I make no secret of the fact that the yew is one of my favourite garden plants. It is without equal as a hedging shrub and for topiary. While one species is grown to the exclusion of almost all others, it is, however, a very variable plant, although the ground cover forms are perhaps the least widely appreciated variants.* ❞❞

■ **CARE** Mulch and apply general fertilizer in spring. All parts are very poisonous.
■ **PROPAGATION** Take hardwood cuttings in winter.
■ **PRUNING** None necessary, although old or overgrown plants may be cut back hard and will regenerate from old wood.

Taxus baccata 'Repens Aurea'

■ **PROBLEMS** Dieback, phytophthora or other root rots.
■ **FEATURES** Evergreen conifers with dark green, dense foliage comprising masses of flattened needles. Golden and variegated forms are available. Yew plants are either male or female, the females producing scarlet fruits.

SIZE Ground cover forms reach about 1 x 1.5m (3 x 5ft) after 5 years, then spread indefinitely but slowly.
SITE AND SOIL Full sun to deep shade, except golden forms, which scorch in direct sun and lose their colour in deep shade. Any well-drained soil, even tolerant of alkaline sites.
Weed Suppression Rating 4–5.
HARDINESS Very hardy, tolerating -20°C (-4°F) or below.

Recommended varieties
There are many forms of *Taxus baccata*, which can differ markedly from the parent: 'Cavendishii' semi-prostrate mound, wide-spreading branches that droop at the tips, female form, less than 1m (3ft) high, spread up to 4m (13ft), 'Repandens' AGM spreading, semi-prostrate, female, very dark green foliage, 30–60cm x 1m (1–2 x 3ft) after 5 years, eventually may spread to 5m (16ft), 'Repens Aurea' low, spreading, female form, leaves with yellow margins when young that later turn cream, loses its colour in deep shade so best sited in some sun, 60–90cm x 1.2–1.5m (2–3 x 4–5ft).

BAMBOOS

Bamboos

" Bamboos, so I am told, are among the more desirable plants for the modern garden. They are, to use a dreadful notion, fashionable. Personally I think that bamboos are misplaced in most temperate gardens and the best of them are also too tender really to be successful. Nonetheless, clearly many people like them, and because they are often rather vigorous there are species that can be used as ground cover. But do remember that this is one group of plants where 'good ground cover' can soon mean 'invasive', and once established any bamboo takes some removing. "

■ **CARE** Prepare the planting position thoroughly with organic matter. Mulch and apply general fertilizer in spring.
■ **PROPAGATION** Sever well-rooted sections and replant in spring or early summer.
■ **PRUNING** Cut out old culms in spring. Use a mattock or sharp spade to chop away the edges of the thicket if it encroaches on other plants.
■ **PROBLEMS** None, but rabbits, squirrels and deer may damage shoots.
■ **FEATURES** Evergreen foliage offers summer features but can look ragged and untidy in winter. Canes are ornamental.

SIZE Most are around 1.5m (5ft) tall, but spread varies greatly.
SITE AND SOIL Most require a sunny site and well-drained soil, but there are exceptions (see Recommended varieties).
Weed Suppression Rating 2.
HARDINESS Forms recommended here are hardy, tolerating at least -15°C (5°F).

Shibataea kumasasa

Sasa veitchii

Pseudosasa japonica

Recommended varieties

Indocalamus tesselatus (syn. *Sasa tessellata*) dense thickets, bright green canes, the leaves are probably the largest among all hardy bamboos, up to 60cm (24in) long and 5–10cm (2–4in) wide, their weight bending the canes down and giving the clumps a dwarf habit, olive-green canes up to 2m (6ft) tall, but once bent down 1 x 1m (3 x 3ft); *Pseudosasa japonica* (syn. *Arundinaria japonica*) AGM clump forming in cooler climates, leaves 25cm (10in) long with a grey underside and green marginal stripe, very hardy, 4 x 1m (13 x 3ft); *Sasa veitchii* running rhizomes form a large thicket, shade tolerant, leaves 20cm (8in) long with blunt tips and remaining attractive all year round, in early autumn they develop a white stripe around their edges, producing a variegated effect that lasts all winter, purple-tinted culms, 1.5 x 1m (5 x 3ft); *Sasaella ramosa* (syn. *Arundinaria vagans*), a short bamboo but very invasive, will grow where little else thrives, even in dense shade, branches horizontally from the middle of the culms, bright green leaves 10-15cm (4-6in) long with downy undersides, foliage may decay at the edges in winter, purple-tinted culms, 1m x 45cm (3ft x 18in); *Shibataea kumasasa* (syn. *Sasa ruscifolia*) clump forming in cooler climates, dark green leaves only 8cm (3in) long, leaves may wither at the tips, canes have a zigzag outline and are pale green ageing to dull brown, best in moist soil, 1.5m x 30cm (5ft x 12in).

GRASSES AND RUSHES

Grasses and Rushes

❝ *As I have mentioned earlier, there is a good argument for considering grass the best of all ground cover plants – there really is no better way of covering ground than by growing a lawn. But it isn't the blanket treatment produced by turf that I have in mind here. Some of the ornamental grasses and their cousins, the rushes, can be used to quite striking effect when planted* en masse. *Don't imagine that you will be achieving an effect comparable to a lawn, however – and you certainly won't create something that can be mown and trampled like a lawn.* ❞

Festuca glauca Blue fescue

■ **CARE** Regular division is necessary to maintain the blue colour.

■ **PROPAGATION** Lift and divide plants in spring every two years. Sow seed in spring or autumn.

■ **TRIMMING** None necessary, but flowers may be removed with shears when they turn brown.

■ **PROBLEMS** None, but can die if soil is waterlogged in winter.

■ **FEATURES** Evergreen, clump-forming grass with blue leaves. Flowers are produced in late spring to early summer.

Festuca glauca

SIZE 20 x 60cm (8 x 24in) after 5 years, 30cm (12in) tall when in flower.
SITE AND SOIL Sunny site and well-drained soil, a good choice for dry or poor situations.
Weed Suppression Rating 1.
HARDINESS Hardy, tolerating -15 to -20°C (5 to -4°F).

Recommended varieties
The species is often used for ground cover, although there are named varieties like 'Blaufuchs' with more intensely blue foliage.

Holcus

■ **CARE** No special care necessary.
■ **PROPAGATION** Divide in spring or cut off rooted runners.
■ **TRIMMING** None necessary, but pull out runners to restrict the spread. May be mown, ideally with a hover mower, if it is well established. Remove seedheads to avoid green-leaved seedlings becoming dominant.

SIZE Each tuft is 15 x 25–30cm (6 x 10–12in), 30cm (12in) tall when in flower, runners make the spread indefinite.
SITE AND SOIL Best in a moist, shady site, but thrives in sun or shade in moist but well-drained soil; unlikely to succeed in a sunny site on poor, dry soil.
Weed Suppression Rating 1.
HARDINESS Hardy, tolerating -15 to -20°C (5 to -4°F).

Holcus mollis **'Albovariegatus'**

■ **PROBLEMS** None.
■ **FEATURES** The smallest of the white-variegated grasses. The main attraction is the foliage, which is best in spring and autumn. Green-white flowers appear in summer but are of little decorative value.

Recommended varieties
Only *Holcus mollis* 'Albovariegatus' (velvet grass) is grown in gardens, tufted grass, spreads by runners, leaves 20cm (8in) long, green with white margins.

Luzula Woodrush

■ **CARE** No special care necessary but don't plant close to a real lawn as I have known it to invade the turf.
■ **PROPAGATION** Lift and divide clumps in spring.

■ **TRIMMING** None necessary.
■ **PROBLEMS** None.
■ **FEATURES** Evergreen, grass-like plant with leaves that are bright yellow in winter but turn green by the middle of summer. Brown flowers are borne in mid-spring to early summer.

SIZE 30-45cm x 1m (12-18in x 3ft) after 5 years.
SITE AND SOIL Tolerates dense shade in either wet or dry soils.
Weed Suppression Rating 1.
HARDINESS Hardy, tolerating -15 to -20°C (5 to -4°F).

Recommended varieties
Luzula sylvatica 'Aurea' (syn. *L. maxima* 'Aurea') bright yellow in winter, mid-green in summer, 'Marginata' (syn. 'Aureomarginata') hairy, broad green leaves with a thin white edge.

PERENNIALS AND ALPINES

Acaena New Zealand burr

❝ Far too many people see acaenas for sale in the alpine section of their garden centre, buy them, and two or three seasons later realize that they have bought a monster, relatively speaking. They are vigorous and hardy, and while I don't think they will ever swamp an entire garden, they will certainly embrace an alpine trough and undoubtedly offer a quick and very attractive way of covering a moderately sized area. ❞

■ **CARE** No special care necessary, but will benefit from an application of general fertilizer in spring. Excessive growth may be clipped back or rooted stems pulled out.

■ **PROPAGATION** Lift and divide in spring, or replant self-rooted stolons. Can also be raised from seed sown in autumn or early spring.

■ **PROBLEMS** None, although may be invasive.

■ **FEATURES** Creeping evergreen perennials, making a dense mat of foliage. Small leaves in interesting colours and colourful burrs (fruits) are the main attractions. The small green-white flowers are insignificant.

SIZE 2.5–15 x 15–90cm (1–6 x 6–36in) after 5 years.
SITE AND SOIL Full sun or partial shade and well-drained soil. Ideal for poor or sandy sites.
Weed Suppression Rating 4–5.
HARDINESS Hardy, tolerating -15 to -20°C (5 to -4°F).

Recommended varieties
Acaena buchananii grey-green leaves, green-yellow burrs in late summer, 2.5 x 75cm (1 x 30in); *A. microphylla* AGM bronze-tinted leaves, bright crimson burrs in late summer, 5 x 15cm (2 x 6in), 'Kupferteppich' (syn. 'Copper Carpet', 'Purple Carpet'), vigorous, 5 x 60cm (2 x 24in), copper-black foliage, red burrs in late summer; *A. novae-zelandiae* (syn. *A. anserinifolia*), bright blue-green leaves, red burrs, 15 x 90cm (6 x 36in).

Acaena novae-zelandiae

Achillea Yarrow

❝ Many gardeners' first (and possibly last) encounter with yarrow is in their lawn. It isn't difficult to control with selective weedkillers, but the very fact that it does establish quickly in turf and is tolerant of being mown and walked on demonstrates that it can form rather effective ornamental ground cover, too. ❞

■ **CARE** Best when lifted and divided every three to four years. Trim back untidy foliage in spring.

■ **PROPAGATION** Lift and divide in autumn or spring. Sow seed in spring or autumn.

■ **PROBLEMS** None, but may be short lived.

■ **FEATURES** Herbaceous and semi-evergreen perennials, some with feathery aromatic foliage. Daisy-like flowers in a range of pastel and hotter colours,

Achillea clavennae

some arranged in flat, plate-like flower-heads, are borne from late spring to summer.

HEIGHT AND SPREAD Varies (see Recommended varieties).
SITE AND SOIL Sunny site, but tolerant of any soil except heavy, wet clay. Good choice for light, dry soils.
Weed Suppression Rating 4.
HARDINESS Hardy, tolerating -15 to -20°C (5 to -4°F).

Recommended varieties
Achillea clavennae (syn. *A. argentea*) mat-like habit, prostrate stems, semi-evergreen, white-hairy foliage, white daisy-like flowers, intolerant of winter wet, 15 x 25cm (6 x 10in); *A. millefolium* named varieties are available in a wide range of flower colours including various shades of red, pink, yellow and cream, foliage is either green or grey-green, 60–75 x 60cm (24–30 x 24in).

Ajuga

" "*The ajugas are among those rather common perennials that create a ground cover effect in gardens unintentionally, having been purchased for their ornamental foliage. The more vigorous forms especially then surprise their owners with their ability to spread. They also tend to surprise their owners with mildew, and this is for me the major drawback to what are otherwise very striking and effective plants.* "

■ **CARE** Prepare the planting position carefully, incorporating organic matter. Pull away any foliage that is disfigured with mildew.
■ **PROPAGATION** Divide clumps in spring; *Ajuga reptans* will produce plantlets from stolons.
■ **PROBLEMS** Powdery mildew.
■ **FEATURES** Creeping, evergreen perennials with colourful leaves and short flower spikes in spring or early summer.

SIZE 10-15 x 45cm (4-6 x 18in) after 5 years.
SITE AND SOIL Sun or shade; varieties differ in where they produce best leaf coloration. Always best in moist but free-draining soil.
Weed Suppression Rating 2–3.
HARDINESS Hardy, tolerating -15 to -20°C (5 to -4°F).

Ajuga reptans '**Catlin's Giant**'

Recommended varieties
Ajuga pyramidalis 'Metallica Crispa' bronze-tinted foliage with crinkled edges, dark blue flowers, divide every two years to maintain vigour, 10 x 45cm (4 x 18in); *A. reptans* (bugle) mat forming with stolons, glossy dark green foliage, short blue flower spikes, 15 x 45cm (6 x 18in), 'Alba' dark green foliage, white flowers, 'Atropurpurea' (syn. 'Purpurea') AGM dark purple leaves with bronze tints, best in sun, 'Braunherz' AGM dark purple shiny foliage, 'Burgundy Glow' AGM, white-green foliage variegated red, 'Catlin's Giant' (syn. 'Macrophylla') AGM vigorous variety with large bronze foliage, 25–30cm (10–12in) tall when in flower, 'Multicolor' (syn. 'Rainbow', 'Tricolor') neat habit, dark brown foliage marked with grey-green and cream, 'Variegata' (syn. 'Argentea') neat habit, grey-green and cream foliage, best in shade.

Alchemilla Lady's mantle

❝ *Superficially, it might seem that a herbaceous perennial that dies back to almost nothing in winter can't be a truly effective ground cover plant. And yet if it is a green carpet to set off summer flowers and suppress weed growth that you need, this plant will perform the task admirably and with enormous charm. It's become a gardening convention to refer to the way that raindrops accumulate on the leaves as 'like beads of mercury' but it is a reasonable simile and also very attractive indeed.* ❞

■ **CARE** Apply general fertilizer in spring. The foliage looks untidy by early winter and is then best trimmed off, to leave mounds from which fresh green leaves will arise in spring.

■ **PROPAGATION** Lift and divide plants in autumn or spring. Sow seed in spring or autumn.
■ **PROBLEMS** None; will self-seed but is rarely invasive.

■ **FEATURES** Easy-to-grow hardy perennials forming low mounds of green leaves that are lobed and rounded. Masses of tiny yellow-green flowers appear in summer.

SIZE 15–50 x 50cm (6–20 x 20in).
SITE AND SOIL Sun or shade and all soils except waterlogged.
Weed Suppression Rating 2–3.
HARDINESS Very hardy, tolerating at least -20°C (-4°F).

Recommended varieties
Alchemilla alpina (alpine lady's mantle) dark green leaves with hairy undersides, flowers held in upright clusters, 15 x 45cm (6 x 18in); *A. xanthochlora* (syn. *A. vulgaris*) European native, yellow-green leaves with hairy undersides, 25–50 x 50cm (10–20 x 20in).

Alyssum

❝ *It's one of gardening and botany's ironies that the two most familiar garden alyssums have moved on to other genera. The mustard-yellow flower that accompanies the reds and mauves of aubrieta on many a garden wall is* Aurinia saxatilis, *the white-flowered bedding plant called sweet alyssum is* Lobularia maritima. *We are left, however, with a group of delightful species of which this alpine ground cover is one of the best.* ❞

■ **CARE** Trim back lightly after flowering to encourage bushy growth.

Alchemilla xanthochlora

■ **PROPAGATION** Take softwood cuttings in late spring to early summer. Sow seed in late summer or autumn.
■ **PROBLEMS** None.
■ **FEATURES** Most are low-growing evergreen perennials grown for their dense clusters of bright yellow, white or pink flowers.

SIZE 8 x 30cm (3 x 12in).
SITE AND SOIL Sunny position and well-drained soil. Good choice for alkaline sites.
Weed Suppression Rating 3.
HARDINESS Hardy, tolerating -15 to -20°C (5 to -4°F)

Recommended varieties
Alyssum serpyllifolium sprawling mat, grey-green to silver foliage, bright yellow flowers.

Anaphalis Pearly everlasting

❝ *By no stretch of the imagination can* Anaphalis *be called a densely growing plant. But there are so many of its rather open, loose-textured stems that collectively they do work rather well in a smothering role, although if it's tidiness you are after I suggest you look elsewhere.* ❞

■ **CARE** Mulch in spring and keep well watered; it flops and wilts if allowed to become too dry.
■ **PROPAGATION** Lift and divide in autumn or spring. Take basal cuttings in

SIZE 60 x 60cm (24 x 24in).
SITE AND SOIL Sun or partial shade. Well-drained soil that does not dry out in summer.
Weed Suppression Rating 1-2
HARDINESS Hardy, tolerating -15 to -20°C (5 to -4°F)

early spring but don't allow leaves to harbour moisture.
■ **PROBLEMS** None.
■ **FEATURES** Unobtrusive herbaceous perennial with grey-green foliage except when flowering in late summer. Flowers are borne in loose clusters and last until early autumn.

Recommended varieties
Anaphalis triplinervis AGM dense clumps of grey-green foliage, clusters of white flowers.

Alyssum serpyllifolium

Anaphalis triplinervis

PERENNIALS AND ALPINES

Antennaria Everlasting

❝ It's alphabetical coincidence that places the plant called 'everlasting' immediately after that called 'pearly everlasting'. They have a botanical connection in both belonging to the daisy family, but there the resemblance ends and I always think this alpine plant bears a rather close similarity to the quite unrelated Armeria *(see p. 64). It is similarly effective at creating a tight, close carpet in limited space.* ❞

■ **CARE** On heavy sites, lighten the soil with grit or organic matter. Apply general fertilizer in spring.
■ **PROPAGATION** Lift and divide in spring. Sow ripe seed in autumn or early winter.

SIZE 10 x 30–60cm (4 x 12–24in).
SITE AND SOIL Full sun and well-drained soil.
Weed Suppression Rating 2.
HARDINESS Hardy, tolerating -15 to -20°C (5 to -4°F).

Recommended varieties
Antennaria dioica (syn. *Gnaphalium dioicum, Omalotheca dioica*) (catsfoot) silver-white mat with dense woolly leaves, white to pink-brown bracts; *A. microphylla* (syn. *A.* var. *rosea*) AGM spreading mat, woolly leaves, pink flowers; *A. parvifolia* (syn. *A. aprica*), silver-grey mat, dense woolly leaves, brown-spotted flower bracts with white or pink tips.

■ **PROBLEMS** None.
■ **FEATURES** Evergreen or semi-evergreen perennials with hairy grey or white leaves. Small clusters of white, pink or red daisy-like flowers are borne in late spring to early summer.

Anthemis

❝ Anthemis *have the classically formed yellow daisy flowers of many another garden perennial. But although, like many other border daisies, they are clump forming, the close basal mat of foliage does form a rather tight, effective soil-covering blanket. Being low growing means that they don't need staking.* ❞

■ **CARE** Apply general fertilizer in spring. Cut back stems after flowering.
■ **PROPAGATION** Divide in autumn or spring. Take basal cuttings in spring or summer.
■ **PROBLEMS** None, but plants may be short lived.
■ **FEATURES** Clump-forming perennials grown for their daisy-like flowers in summer and finely divided, sometimes aromatic foliage.

SIZE 30–60 x 60cm (12–24 x 24in).
SITE AND SOIL Open, sunny site and well-drained soil.
Weed Suppression Rating 2–3.
HARDINESS Varies (see Recommended varieties).

Anthemis tinctoria **'Wargrave Variety'**

Recommended varieties

Anthemis punctata subsp. *cupaniana* AGM mound-like habit, aromatic grey foliage, white flowers with yellow centres, main flowering in early summer and then intermittently until autumn, fairly hardy, tolerating about -10°C (14°F), 30 x 60cm (12 x 24in); *A. tinctoria* 'Wargrave Variety', mid-green fern-like foliage, very pale yellow flowers from early to late summer, hardy, tolerating down to -15°C (5°F), 60 x 60cm (24 x 24in).

Arabis Rock cress

❝ Some years ago, when restoring a neglected cottage garden, I first realized just how vigorous these white-flowered alpines can be. What had once been a single small plant had swamped a low boundary wall and taken over a fair part of the adjoining garden, too. In similar conditions, it would do the same for you. ❞

■ **CARE** Apply general fertilizer in spring. Trim lightly after flowering to encourage a bushy habit.

■ **PROPAGATION** Take softwood cuttings in summer or divide established plants after flowering. Species come true from seed – sow in spring or autumn.

■ **PROBLEMS** Aphids, downy mildew.

■ **FEATURES** Evergreen perennials.

Arabis alpina subsp. *caucasica* 'Schneehaube'

forming dense mats of foliage, with clusters of small white flowers in spring or summer. Robust plants, but they may be invasive.

SIZE 15–25 x 45–50cm (6–10 x 18–20in).
SITE AND SOIL Sunny site and well-drained soil. Tolerates hot, dry conditions and poor soils.
Weed Suppression Rating 3–4.
HARDINESS Moderately hardy to hardy, tolerating about -15°C (5°F)

Recommended varieties

Arabis alpina subsp. *caucasica* 'Schneehaube' (syn. *A. albida*, *A. billardieri* 'Snowcap') AGM mat-forming evergreen, more compact than the species, white flowers in spring, 'Variegata' white or very pale yellow edges to the leaves; *A. procurrens* dense flat mat, white flowers in spring, 'Old Gold', smaller with shiny leaves with green and gold variegations, white flowers.

Armeria Thrift

❝ *There are areas of sea cliff where you can walk for many metres, if not kilometres, over a light springy turf composed almost entirely of* Armeria maritima. *It comes as close as almost any plant I know to mimicking the texture and durability of real grass turf, although you shouldn't imagine that it can be mown. It really does grow best in coastal gardens.* ❞

■ **CARE** Apply general fertilizer in spring. Trim off dead flowerheads for tidiness.
■ **PROPAGATION** Divide established plants in spring or autumn, or take semi-ripe basal cuttings in summer. Sow seed of species in autumn or early winter.

■ **PROBLEMS** None.
■ **FEATURES** Evergreen perennials, which form neat tufts or cushions of foliage. Globular flowerheads in pink, red or white are held on erect stems above the foliage in early summer.

SIZE 20 x 30–50cm (8 x 12–20in).
SITE AND SOIL Full sun and any well-drained soil. Ideal for coastal areas.
Weed Suppression Rating 3–4.
HARDINESS Very hardy, tolerating -20°C (-4°F)

Recommended varieties
Armeria maritima (syn. *A. vulgaris*; sea thrift) dark green foliage, white or deep pink flowers from late spring to summer, 'Alba' large white flowerheads on short stalks.

Asarum Wild ginger

❝ *Don't let the name mislead you into thinking that this is a plant for the kitchen. It isn't the source of culinary ginger, although it has been used as a substitute for ginger and also for medicinal purposes. I would rather you used it as a substitute for bare soil in shady, moist places where the rather large and glossy dark green leaves combine to produce an extremely attractive foliage carpet. It looks tropical and tender, but isn't.* ❞

■ **CARE** Apply general fertilizer in spring. Mulch with garden compost or leaf mould to maintain moisture in the soil.
■ **PROPAGATION** Lift and divide established plants in spring. Sow seed in a cold frame in autumn.

SIZE 10–15 x 40–50cm (4–6 x 16–20in).
SITE AND SOIL These woodland plants grow best in shady areas, in moist, acidic or neutral soil.
Weed Suppression Rating 2.
HARDINESS Hardy, tolerating -15 to -20°C (5 to -4°F).

Recommended varieties
Asarum caudatum spreading evergreen, heart-shaped, hairy leaves up to 15cm (6in) long; *A. europaeum* (asarabacca) creeping, rhizomatous plant with evergreen, shiny, kidney-shaped leaves up to 12cm (5in) wide, best in deep shade.

Armeria maritima

■ **PROBLEMS** Slugs, snails.

■ **FEATURES** Fairly low-growing herbaceous perennials whose main feature is their glossy, deep green leaves. There are bronze-purple flowers in late winter to early spring, but they are hidden by the foliage. The rhizomes smell of ginger.

Bergenia Elephant's ears

❝ *A border perennial much loved by the blessed Miss Gertrude Jekyll. Although some varieties do produce quite striking spikes of brightly coloured flowers, I never think this is a plant of great beauty. Nor is it as drought or shade tolerant as is sometimes claimed. But, as its common names implies, it does produce rather enormous leaves that will suppress almost anything that dares to try to grow beneath them.* ❞

■ **CARE** Apply general fertilizer in spring and cut away dead or winter-damaged leaves.

■ **PROPAGATION** Divide in autumn or spring. Sow seed in a cold frame in spring.

■ **PROBLEMS** Leaf spot, vine weevil.

■ **FEATURES** Evergreen perennials with rhizome-like, prostrate stems and clumps of glossy, large, rounded leaves. Some varieties have attractive winter foliage tints. Early-spring flowers are borne in loose clusters; the flower colours vary but are generally pink, white or red.

SIZE Varies, but around 45 x 45–60cm (18 x 18–24in).

SITE AND SOIL Full sun or moderate shade and most soils. Ideal for inhospitable sites, coping well with neglect, but avoid frost pockets as frost can damage early flowers and some species have leaves that die back in winter and lose ground cover effect.

Weed Suppression Rating 3–4.

HARDINESS Varies, but most are hardy, tolerating -15 to -20°C (5 to -4°F)

Recommended varieties
'Ballawley' semi-evergreen, less hardy than most, rose-pink flowers, can reach 60cm (24in) tall; *B. cordifolia* AGM leathery round leaves up to 25cm (10in) across, pink flowers, 'Purpurea' AGM leaves turn purple in winter, dark purple flowers in spring; 'Sunningdale' mid-green leaves that turn bronze in winter, rose-pink flowers on red stems; 'Wintermärchen' small, shiny leaves that turn bright red in winter, rose-red flowers on red stems.

Bergenia cordifolia **'Purpurea'**

Brunnera

❝ *Brunneras aren't forget-me-nots, despite the close resemblance between the flowers. They are, however, in the same family, but it is the difference in their leaves that makes brunneras good ground cover while forget-me-nots (with one exception, see p. 78) aren't. Their real drawback is that their foliage is very prone to winter browning.* ❞

■ **CARE** Mulch and apply general fertilizer in early spring. Trim back old flower spikes as they fade. Cut off any leaves browned at the edges by the cold. Cut out any all-green shoots on variegated varieties.

■ **PROPAGATION** Lift and divide in autumn or spring. Take root cuttings in early spring. Some forms may be raised from seed sown in early summer.

■ **PROBLEMS** None.

■ **FEATURES** Herbaceous perennials with heart-shaped leaves. In spring, sprays of flowers appear that are similar to forget-me-nots.

Brunnera 'Hadspen Cream'

SIZE 40 x 60cm (16 x 20in).
SITE AND SOIL Shade is ideal, but tolerates sun if the soil does not dry out. Prefers cool, moist soil enriched with organic matter, otherwise plants tend to look unkempt. Protect from cold winds or foliage can turn brown.
Weed Suppression Rating 2–3.
HARDINESS Hardy, tolerating -15 to -20°C (5 to -4°F)

Recommended varieties
Brunnera macrophylla (syn. *Anchusa myosotidiflora*) AGM heart-shaped, mid-green foliage, wiry stems holding tiny blue flowers in spring, 'Aluminium Spot' (syn. 'Langtrees') green leaves with silver-white spots, 'Dawson's White' (syn. 'Variegata') white and green variegated foliage, 'Hadspen Cream' AGM light green leaves edged with cream.

Campanula Bellflower

❝ *Campanula is a big genus (over 300 species) of plants united in their possession of usually blue, bell-shaped flowers. In habit, however, they range widely, from tall, lax border perennials that suffer from flopping more than almost any other plant I know, to low-growing, extremely invasive rock garden species that will subjugate all around them. And in between comes* Campanula glomerata, *a plant that will gradually take over a border more charmingly and with more subtlety than almost any other.* ❞

■ **CARE** Mulch and apply general fertilizer in spring. Trim back old flower spikes as they fade and cut off any leaves browned by cold.

■ **PROPAGATION** Divide in autumn or spring. Forms with long underground runners may be lifted and rooted sections cut off. Some forms can be raised from seed sown in early summer in a cold frame.

■ **PROBLEMS** Slugs, snails.

■ **FEATURES** Large genus, all the

Campanula rapunculoides

members having bell-shaped flowers in blue or white, sometimes pink. Habits vary greatly.

SIZE Varies greatly (see Recommended varieties).
SITE AND SOIL Most are easy to grow in sun or semi-shade and moist but well-drained soil.
Weed Suppression Rating 4.
HARDINESS Very hardy, tolerating -20°C (-4°F) or below, although evergreen rosettes may be browned by cold winds.

Recommended Varieties
Campanula glomerata vigorous rhizomatous perennial that may be invasive, deep green leaves, rounded heads of small purple flowers in summer, 45 x 80cm (18 x 32in); *C. portenschlagiana* (syn. *C. muralis*; Dalmatian bellflower) AGM spreading evergreen, deep lavender-blue flowers in summer, can be very invasive and one of the most curious recipients of an AGM, 15 x 50cm (6 x 20in); *C. poscharskyana* spreading evergreen, pale green leaves, star-like violet-blue flowers in summer and early autumn, 10–15 x 60cm (4–6 x 24in); *C. rapunculoides* (creeping bellflower) rhizomatous perennial, invasive, deep green leaves, wiry stems with dainty blue flowers in summer and early autumn, may naturalize in grass, 45 x 45cm (18 x 18in); *C. takesimana* spreading rhizomatous perennial, bright green leaves arranged in rosettes, arching sprays of white bells in summer, 60 x 50cm (24 x 20in).

Chamaemelum Camomile

❝ *Of all the plants that gardeners have heard about and want to grow as a substitute for a grass lawn, this is the most famous. However, as I have said in several places in this book, there is no real, practical alternative to grass – but that is no reason for not growing a small area of camomile for its ground-covering qualities and simple, soft, aromatic charm.* ❞

■ **CARE** Apply a light dressing of general fertilizer in spring. Best divided or raised from cuttings every two or three years to prevent the plants from becoming unkempt or dying back. Remove faded flowers and clip the foliage to maintain bushiness.
■ **PROPAGATION** Divide in spring or sow seed of species in summer.

Take semi-ripe cuttings of the flowerless 'Treneague' in late spring or late summer.
■ **PROBLEMS** None.
■ **FEATURES** Evergreen perennials with soft, feathery, aromatic foliage above which small daisy-like flowers are borne.

SIZE 10–25 x 30–45cm (4–10 x 12–18in).
SITE AND SOIL Full sun in a sheltered spot and light but well-drained soil.
Weed Suppression Rating 3–4.
HARDINESS Moderately hardy to hardy, tolerating around -15°C (-4°F) but browned by cold winds.

Recommended varieties
Chamaemelum nobile (syn. *Anthemis nobilis*) bright green leaves, white flowers with yellow centres, 25 x 45cm (10 x 18in), 'Flore Pleno' double white flowers, 15 x 30cm (6 x 12in), 'Treneague' non-flowering form often used on a small scale to produce an alternative 'lawn', 10 x 30cm (4 x 12in).

Chamaemelum nobile

PERENNIALS AND ALPINES

Chrysogonum Golden star

❝ *One of the lesser known among yellow daisies but, like a number of other yellow-flowered perennials, rather shade tolerant – perhaps yellow flowers show through the gloom and so insects can still find them. In milder areas or seasons it will retain its foliage through the winter, and all in all this is a very desirable and unjustifiably little known plant.* ❞

■ **CARE** Apply a mulch and general fertilizer in spring. Give protection in the first winter in cold areas.
■ **PROPAGATION** Divide in spring or summer. Sow ripe seed in autumn.
■ **PROBLEMS** None.
■ **FEATURES** Spreading rhizomatous perennials with single, golden yellow, single daisy flowers and bright green foliage.

SIZE 25 x 60cm (10 x 24in).
SITE AND SOIL Best in moist but well-drained soil in damp, shady places; good woodland edge plant.
Weed Suppression Rating 3.
HARDINESS Moderately hardy, tolerating about -15°C (5°F).

Recommended varieties
Chrysogonum virginianum oval, hairy, bright green leaves, single five-petalled flowers with yellow centres throughout the summer.

Dianthus Pink

❝ *Florists' carnations, with their huge, ungainly heads and ridiculous colours, are among the flowers that I really do not like. And yet their genus,* Dianthus, *includes some of the prettiest and most charming of species. Among them are some mat-forming plants that, given the scope of a fairly large rock garden, small border or paved area, will provide an endearing and enduring carpet.* ❞

■ **CARE** Apply general fertilizer in spring.
■ **PROPAGATION** Take cuttings of non-flowering shoots in summer. Sow seed of species in autumn or winter and keep in a cold frame over winter. Some of the tufted forms may be divided after flowering or in spring.
■ **PROBLEMS** None.
■ **FEATURES** Large genus with ever-green, mostly grey-green or blue-grey foliage. Flowers vary from simple five-petalled single flowers to fully double florists' carnations; most are scented with a delightful spicy fragrance. The

SIZE Forms recommended here are both 15 x 30cm (6 x 12in).
SITE AND SOIL Open, sunny site and well-drained soil that is neutral or slightly alkaline. Tolerant of salt winds and pollution.
Weed Suppression Rating 2–3.
HARDINESS Hardy, tolerating -15 to -20°C (5 to -4°F)

Dianthus gratianopolitanus

ground cover forms recommended here are hardy and perennial, with single flowers.

Epimedium

❝ For plants with long, rather wiry leaf stalks and seemingly fragile leaves, epimediums create extremely dense cover, a result of the foliage developing in multiple layers. The leaves are thin, however, and while the plants are hardy enough, the foliage may brown in places exposed to cold winds. ❞

Epimedium x *cantabrigiense*

■ **CARE** Mulch well with garden compost or leaf mould and apply general fertilizer in spring. Trim away old foliage in early spring to make way for new growth.

■ **PROPAGATION** Lift and divide in spring. Take semi-ripe cuttings in late summer. Sow ripe seed of species in late summer.

■ **PROBLEMS** None.

■ **FEATURES** Deciduous or evergreen perennials grown mostly for their foliage, which provides dense cover and is often attractively tinted. Some species have good spring flowers.

SIZE Varies; forms recommended here are under 50 x 60cm (20 x 24in).
SITE AND SOIL Partial or full shade, as sun can scorch foliage. Moist but well-drained soil preferred, as is some shelter from cold winds and hard frosts as the foliage may brown unattractively.
Weed Suppression Rating 3.
HARDINESS Very hardy, tolerating -20°C (-4°F)

PERENNIALS AND ALPINES

Erigeron Fleabane

❝ I don't know if this little Mexican species was ever the bane of fleas, like some of its European relatives, but it is among the few plants from that part of the world that are not only fully hardy in cooler climates but can even become slightly invasive. It is so charming, however, that no one could surely ever think ill of it. ❞

■ **CARE** Apply general fertilizer in spring.

■ **PROPAGATION** Self-seeds so will spread readily, but can also be divided or softwood basal cuttings taken in spring. Sow seed in spring or autumn.

■ **PROBLEMS** None, apart from the propensity to self-seed to some distance.

■ **FEATURES** Herbaceous perennials grown for their long-lasting, daisy-like flowers.

> SIZE *Erigeron karvinskianus* reaches 15 x 40cm (6 x 16in).
> **SITE AND SOIL** Full sun and well-drained soil.
> **Weed Suppression Rating 1–2.**
> **HARDINESS** Very hardy, tolerating -20°C (-4°F) or below.

> **Recommended varieties**
> *Erigeron karvinskianus* (syn. *E. mucronatus*; wall daisy) AGM low-growing, dies down in winter, grey-green leaves, daisy flowers from early summer to autumn that are first white, then change to pink and then purple, may be invasive but seldom aggressively so.

Erigeron karvinskianus

Euphorbia Spurge

❝ Euphorbias were among the great plants of the latter part of the twentieth century and there's no reason to suppose that their popularity won't continue well into the twenty-first. They offer a wide variety of overall size and shape, although a relative uniformity in flower structure and colour. However, they include one species that, while never a thing of the utmost beauty, will certainly spread reliably wherever it is planted. ❞

■ **CARE** Mulch and apply general fertilizer in early spring. Cut down old flowering stems as they fade. Over large areas, a powered trimmer may be used in spring to stimulate new growth.

■ **PROPAGATION** Various methods, but not all may be used for all forms. For evergreens like *Euphorbia amygdaloides* var. *robbiae*, take softwood cuttings in late spring or early summer.

■ **PROBLEMS** None.

■ **FEATURES** Euphorbias vary considerably in size, habit and site requirements. The form recommended here is

> SIZE *Euphorbia amygdaloides* var. *robbiae* 30-50 x 30-50cm (12-20 x 12-20in) for individual plants, but spreads further by runners.
> **SITE AND SOIL** Full sun to deep shade. Almost any soil, even very dry.
> **Weed Suppression Rating 3.**
> **HARDINESS** Very hardy, tolerating -20°C (-4°F) or below, but browned in really severe weather.

an evergreen perennial, less showy than some but valuable for its tolerance of shade and dry soil. It unfurls like a fern to reveal yellow-green bracts on thin stems, above very dark green leaf rosettes.

Recommended varieties
Euphorbia amygdaloides var. *robbiae* (syn. *E. robbiae*) evergreen, rapidly spreading rhizomes that are undeniably invasive, green-yellow flowerheads.

Euphorbia amygdaloides var. *robbiae*

Helleborus Hellebore

❝ *Like euphorbias (left), hellebores, too, have been among the success stories of our gardening time. The genus* Helleborus *offers rather more variety than* Euphorbia *in flower colour, and while most are relatively ungainly, clump-forming perennials there is one, very variable species that is an excellent ground cover plant for lightly shaded places – but do be ruthless in tidying it up each season for the best effect.* ❞

■ **CARE** Mulch and apply general fertilizer in spring. Cut down old foliage as it discolours in late winter; this will serve to set off the newly emerging flowers.
■ **PROPAGATION** Take basal cuttings in spring or divide in spring or autumn. Self-sown seedlings will be found under parent plants; *Helleborus orientalis* does not come true from seed.
■ **PROBLEMS** Aphids, leaf spot, stem basal rot.
■ **FEATURES** Herbaceous and evergreen perennials, with green divided leaves. They are valued for their winter and early-spring flowers that are both attractive and long lasting.

SIZE 45 x 45cm (18 x 18in).
SITE AND SOIL Shade preferred, but tolerates sun if soil is moist. Ideal soil is moist loam with plenty of organic matter, but will grow in any except waterlogged.
Weed Suppression Rating 3–4.
HARDINESS Very hardy, tolerating at least -20°C (-4°F).

Recommended varieties
Helleborus orientalis (Lenten rose) more or less evergreen, saucer-shaped flowers from late winter to early spring in colours ranging from white, pink and mauve to deep purple, many with attractive markings.

Helleborus orientalis

Geranium

" The hardy geranium is a mainstay of the flower border in summer, and the many beautiful blue and other coloured varieties derived from wild species are essentially tall, floppy things – and, generally, plants of the sun. But Geranium is a big genus, and it includes low-growing, wide-spreading varieties as well as a few that are shade tolerant. My garden would be very much the poorer without them all. "

■ CARE Little necessary, and I believe geraniums are ideal low-maintenance plants. A general fertilizer may be given in spring to encourage rapid growth and quick cover. Try to cut back dead flowering stems if practical for a tidier effect and to help stimulate a second flush of late-season flowers.

■ PROPAGATION Division is the easiest method, in spring or autumn; only the species come true from seed which should be sown in autumn.

■ PROBLEMS None, although *Geranium* x *oxonianum* 'Claridge Druce' is a rather large plant that self-seeds very freely to some distance and may be a nuisance in small gardens. *G. himalayense* 'Plenum' is often attacked by small, leaf-eating beetles which leave the foliage looking like lace curtains.

■ FEATURES Large genus of attractive and dependable plants, offering beautiful flowers and mounds of dainty foliage, sometimes with autumn tints. Ideal ground cover under roses, between other shrubs or at the front of a border.

SIZE 30 x 60cm (12 x 24in), although some newer introductions are only 15cm (6in) tall.
SITE AND SOIL Most tolerate sun or light shade and most garden soils. A few, like *G. macrorrhizum*, tolerate problem areas like dry shade, while some flower better in full sun.
Weed Suppression Rating 3.
HARDINESS Very hardy, tolerating -20°C (-4°F) unless otherwise stated.

Geranium himalayense

Recommended varieties

Geranium himalayense (syns. *G. grandiflorum*, *G. h.* var. *meeboldii*) perhaps the largest-flowered species, deep violet-blue flowers, dark green foliage, 'Plenum' (syn. *G. h.* 'Birch Double') double purple flowers, less vigorous than single forms; *G. macrorrhizum* (syn. *G. m.* var. *roseum*), pink to purple or white flowers, light green foliage that is aromatic and semi-evergreen with autumn tints, 'Bevan's Variety' deep magenta with red sepals, 'Ingwersen's Variety' AGM soft rose-pink flowers, pale green, slightly glossy foliage, 'Variegatum' pink flowers, grey-green foliage with cream markings; *G.* x *magnificum* (syns. *G. ibericum* var. *platypetalum*) AGM violet-blue with darker veins, free flowering, foliage has autumn tints, often sold under the name of its parents (see synonyms); *G.* x *oxonianum* 'Claridge Druce' deep rose-pink flowers with darker veins, foliage is dark green and evergreen, a self-seeder and vigorous, at least 45–60 x 60cm (18–24 x 24in); *G.* x *riversleaianum* 'Russell Prichard' AGM bright magenta-pink, long flowering, small grey-green foliage, hardy, tolerating -15°C (5°F) but protect the crown in cold areas, best in full sun, 25–45 x 90cm (10–18 x 36in); *G. tuberosum* needs a sunny site with good drainage, ideal for a large rock garden, drought-tolerant plant that flowers in early summer and is then dormant until the following spring, moderately hardy, tolerating -10 to -15°C (14 to 5°F), only 20–25cm (8–10in) tall.

Geranium macrorrhizum **'Ingwersen's Variety'**

Geranium x *riversleaianum* **'Russell Pritchard'**

Heuchera Coal bells

❝ Heucheras are plants too often described (and I've been guilty of this) as useful rather than beautiful. Yet when you look closely at those delicate, wavy flowerheads, held above really rather fine foliage, you have to concede that they have an individual charm. And that foliage does spread to produce quite a convincing ground-covering carpet. ❞

■ **CARE** Mulch and apply general fertilizer in spring, and divide regularly every two years in autumn.

■ **PROPAGATION** By division.

■ **PROBLEMS** Leafy gall, vine weevil.

■ **FEATURES** Evergreen perennials with spreading, woody rhizomes. The main feature is the leaves in striking colours including metallic hues, the shape varying from rounded or lobed to gently scalloped. In summer sprays of small red, pink or white flowers are borne on wiry stems held above the foliage.

SIZE 30 x 35cm (12 x 14in), up to 45–60cm (18-24in) tall when in flower.

SITE AND SOIL Sun or light shade. Well-drained but fertile soil is best, dig in organic matter if it is thin and poor.

Weed Suppression Rating 3.

HARDINESS Very hardy, tolerating at least -20°C (-4°F).

Recommended varieties
'Bressingham Hybrids' rounded leaves with silver mottling and purple tints, white, pink or red flowers; 'Chocolate Ruffles' large brown and burgundy leaves; 'Green Ivory' midgreen to silver foliage, green-white flowers, a tall form, up to 60–75cm (24–30in); 'Persian Carpet' large red and purple foliage; 'Pewter Moon' grey-silver foliage with deep maroon undersides, pale pink flowers.

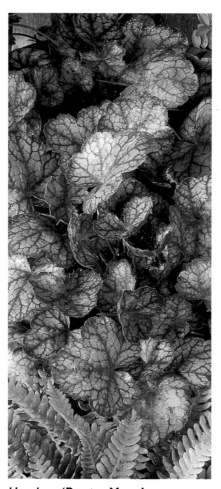

Heuchera 'Pewter Moon'

Hosta

❝ If only the slugs (and snails) would leave them alone, hostas could be the foliage perennials of all time. As it is, in most gardens the molluscs don't leave them alone and if you want to grow hostas as specimen plants, you grow them in containers. Which doesn't, of course, do anything for their role as ground cover plants, for which you must first find a slug- and snail-free garden. ❞

■ **CARE** Mulch in spring and apply general fertilizer.

■ **PROPAGATION** Divide in autumn or spring.

■ **PRUNING** Cut down old flowering stems as soon as they fade. Pull away dead leaves in autumn.

■ **PROBLEMS** Slugs, snails, leaf scorch.

■ **FEATURES** Herbaceous perennials

Hosta sieboldiana var. *elegans*

valued for their bold clumps of foliage. There is a wide range of leaf colour, size, shape and texture, some are rather upright in habit but almost all are potentially effective ground cover plants. Bell-shaped lilac or white flowers are borne in summer.

SIZE Varies, but forms recommended here are 60 x 60–90cm (24 x 24–36in) unless otherwise stated.
SITE AND SOIL Ideally light to moderate shade, but some can tolerate sun if the ground is moist. Soil should be rich and moist.
Weed Suppression Rating 4–5.
HARDINESS Hardy to very hardy, tolerating at least -15°C (5°F)

Recommended varieties
'Big Daddy' rounded leaves, blue with puckered texture; 'Francee' AGM heart-shaped leaves, green with white edges, best in light shade; 'Frances Williams' AGM thick, puckered, heart-shaped leaves, blue-green with yellow edges, best in full shade; 'Gold Standard' AGM oval to heart-shaped leaves, dark green with yellow-green margins then golden yellow, best in light shade; 'Shade Fanfare' AGM glossy oval leaves, deep green with creamy white margins, some puckering, 40 x 60cm (16 x 24in); *Hosta sieboldiana* var. *elegans* AGM large blue-grey leaves that are thick and puckered; 'Sum and Substance' AGM yellow leaves, best in sun, claimed to be slug-tolerant; *H. ventricosa* AGM shiny, heart-shaped dark green leaves, thin foliage so best in shade.

Houttuynia

❝ *If you like the soil in your garden covered with more than a passing resemblance to a Persian rug, then this is the plant for you. If, like me, you prefer your leaves to be more or less green rather than the colours of the rainbow, I suggest you select something else. And you will, in any event, need a moist soil.* ❞

■ **CARE** Mulch and apply general fertilizer in early spring.
■ **PROPAGATION** Divide rhizomes in spring.
■ **PROBLEMS** May be invasive. Leaves can revert to green if grown in shade.
■ **FEATURES** Evergreen perennials with heart-shaped leaves that release a lemon scent when crushed. The cultivar 'Chameleon' has multi-coloured foliage. The inconspicuous summer flowers have white bracts.

SIZE 20cm (8in) x indefinite, 45cm (18in) tall when in flower.
SITE AND SOIL Sunny site for most colourful foliage. Cool, moist soil for most vigorous growth, but will grow slowly in dry sites.
Weed Suppression Rating 3.
HARDINESS Hardy, tolerating -15 to -20°C (5 to -4°F).

Recommended varieties
Houttuynia cordata 'Chameleon' (syn. 'Tricolor') bright foliage with green leaves edged with red and yellow, white flower bracts in summer.

Houttuynia cordata **'Chameleon'**

Lamium Deadnettle

❝ *Most of the deadnettles with which gardeners are familiar are annual weeds of the vegetable garden. Those varieties I recommend here are perennial, not weedy, and are rather lovely for about three-quarters of the season, after which they can become a bit untidy. They are not perhaps, therefore, plants for the most prime of positions.* ❞

■ **CARE** Little care necessary, although general fertilizer may be applied in spring.

■ **PROPAGATION** Divide in autumn or spring. Sow seed or take stem-tip cuttings in summer.

■ **PRUNING** Untidy foliage may be cut back hard after flowering, when new fresh leaves will appear.

■ **PROBLEMS** Leaf-eating beetles, leaf spot, mildew.

■ **FEATURES** Evergreen perennials grown for their lovely foliage, often with pretty silver or gold markings. The

SIZE *L. galeobdolon* 20–30 x 60cm (8–12 x 24in), *L. maculatum* is more wide spreading at 15–20 x 1m (6–8in x 3ft).
SITE AND SOIL Best in light shade but will tolerate sun. Thrives in most soils so good for poor, dry sites.
Weed Suppression Rating 2–3.
HARDINESS Very hardy, tolerating at least -20°C (-4°F).

leaves are at their best from spring to autumn. In some varieties, the flowers are a bonus as they are long lasting, from late spring to early summer.

Recommended varieties
Lamium galeobdolon (syn. *Galeobdolon luteum, Lamiastrum galeobdolon;* yellow archangel) evergreen with heart-shaped leaves, yellow flowers, 'Herman's Pride' narrow, toothed leaves streaked with silver, rarely flowers, 'Silberteppich' (syn. 'Silver Carpet') more clump-like than spreading, silver foliage, rarely flowers; *L. maculatum* central white stripe on green leaves, red or purple flowers, 'Aureum' gold leaves with white stripe, pink flowers, 'Pink Pewter' silver variegations, pale pink flowers, 'Roseum' (syn. 'Shell Pink') white-striped leaves, pale pink flowers, 'White Nancy' AGM silver leaves with green edges, white flowers.

Lamium galeobdolon 'Silberteppich'

Lysimachia Loosestrife

❝ Lysimachia *is one of the more maligned genera of the herbaceous border – maligned because the tall perennials are just too easy to grow for many people's liking. Personally, I like them and find them very useful, but not perhaps as useful or as pretty as this delightful low-growing relative. If there is anything more pleasing than finding it covering the soil and rocks in someone's garden, it can only be finding it doing the same by a natural stream.* ❞

CARE No special care necessary, but benefits from general fertilizer in spring. They will grow in any soil and prefer fertile, moist ground.

SIZE *L. nummularia* reaches 5 x 40cm (2 x 16in).
SITE AND SOIL Sun or shade. Many forms fairly tolerant of dryness, but ground cover form is naturally a streamside plant and best in damp conditions.
Weed Suppression Rating 3.
HARDINESS Very hardy, tolerating at least -20°C (-4°F).

■ **PROPAGATION** Divide in autumn or spring. Sow seed in spring.
■ **PROBLEMS** None.
■ **FEATURES** Diverse genus with species varying greatly in size and habit. The ground cover form recommended here is evergreen and somewhat invasive, with early summer flowers.

Recommended varieties
Lysimachia nummularia (creeping Jenny) prostrate, bright green leaves, yellow flowers, 'Aurea' gold-leaved variant but needs sun to retain its colour.

ysimachia nummularia

Mentha Mint

" The aroma of mint is one of the delights of any herb garden, and if I had to choose from among a dozen or more that the genus Mentha *offers, I think it would be the clear freshness of peppermint. This most diminutive member of the group, of no value as a herb, has peppermint to excess, and its leaves create a velvet-like mat from which fragrance erupts as you walk. "*

■ **CARE** No special care necessary, but benefits from general fertilizer in spring.
■ **PROPAGATION** Portions of the runners will root easily. Plants may also be divided in spring or autumn.
■ **PROBLEMS** Rust.
■ **FEATURES** Aromatic, rhizomatous perennials grown for their foliage. The species recommended here is a miniature gem with minute leaves and tiny summer flowers.

SIZE *M. requienii* 1cm (½in) x indefinite.
SITE AND SOIL Best in light shade and damp soil.
Weed Suppression Rating 4.
HARDINESS Hardy, tolerating -15 to -20°C (5 to -4°F).

Recommended varieties
Mentha requienii (syn. *M. corsica*; Corsican mint) mat of creeping stems, minute bright green leaves with peppermint aroma, extremely tiny lilac flowers.

Mimulus Monkey flower

❝ Mimulus *are loose-growing, often assertively coloured and rather unkempt plants. Not obvious choices, therefore, to enhance any garden, but many people adore them, and if you want bright and cheerful ground cover in a bog garden or similar wet place,* Mimulus *will probably provide it better than most things.* ❞

■ **CARE** Mulch and apply general fertilizer in spring.

■ **PROPAGATION** Easily raised from seed sown in autumn or spring. May also be lifted and divided in spring, or softwood cuttings can be taken in summer.

■ **PROBLEMS** None.

■ **FEATURES** Herbaceous and short-lived perennials grown for their summer flowers. Each tubular flower has two lips and a pouch, and attracts bees and other insects.

SIZE Garden hybrids 30 x 40cm (12 x 16in), *M. primuloides* 10 x 50cm (4 x 20in).
SITE AND SOIL Light shade and preferably moist or wet, slightly acidic soil rich in organic matter.
Weed Suppression Rating 2.
HARDINESS Garden hybrids tolerate -5°C (23°F), *M. primuloides* down to -15°C (5°F).

Recommended varieties
Mimulus garden hybrids are tender perennials often grown as annuals, flower colours in various shades of red, orange and yellow, often with attractive markings; *M. primuloides* herbaceous perennial, spreading habit, light to mid-green leaves, small yellow flowers.

Mimulus primuloides

Myosotis Forget-me-not

❝ *Although I have compared* Myosotis, *the forget-me-nots, unfavourably with* Brunnera *(see p. 66), there is one exception that is worth growing if you have a wet garden. It isn't a neat and tidy plant, and doesn't have large and showy flowers. Nor does it have large and showy leaves, but massed together, foliage and stems do produce a reasonably effective smothering tangle.* ❞

■ **CARE** Cut back dead stems in autumn.
■ **PROPAGATION** Divide in spring. The species may be bulked up by removing self-sown seedlings.

■ **PROBLEMS** Mildew, aphids.
■ **FEATURES** A water garden version of the familiar forget-me-not, with a creeping but not invasive habit. It has small, hairy, bright green leaves and small blue flowers in summer. Deciduous, it retains its foliage in all except the coldest weather.

Myosotis scorpioides

SIZE *M. scorpioides* 25cm x 1m (10in x 3ft).
SITE AND SOIL Full sun to moderate shade and moist or boggy soil.
Weed Suppression Rating 2.
HARDINESS Very hardy, tolerating -20°C (-4°F).

Recommended varieties
Myosotis scorpioides (syn. *M. palustris*; water forget-me-not) rhizomatous, loose habit, hairy leaves, sky-blue flowers with a yellow centre.

Nandina Sacred bamboo

❝ *I have said that bamboos have a good many drawbacks for gardens in temperate climates (see p. 54), but I have often recommended this, quite unrelated plant, as one to produce a somewhat similar effect if you do want something reliably hardy that will impart an Oriental feel.* ❞

■ **CARE** Mulch lightly and apply general fertilizer in spring, and cut back old or winter-damaged shoots to soil level.
■ **PROPAGATION** Divide plants in spring, sow seed in autumn or take softwood cuttings in late summer or early autumn.
■ **PROBLEMS** None.
■ **FEATURES** Looks superficially like a small bamboo, but is really a member of the Berberis family. Grown for its semi-evergreen or evergreen foliage, there are also arching heads of flowers in summer and sometimes fruits.

SIZE *N. domestica* 80 x 80cm (32 x 32in) after 5 years, then slowly reaches 1.5 x 1.5m (5 x 5ft) after 10 years.
SITE AND SOIL Sun or light shade in a sheltered position. Thrives in most garden soils but intolerant of very heavy, wet conditions.
Weed Suppression Rating 2–3.
HARDINESS Hardy, tolerating about -15°C (5°F).

Recommended varieties
Nandina domestica AGM clump of leafy stems, foliage with red-green leaves that turn a strong red-orange in autumn, large sprays of creamy white flowers in summer, red fruits in hot summers and when several plants are grown together.

Nandina domestica

Nepeta

❝ *The name* Nepeta *is most commonly used for a long, trailing plant extensively grown in hanging baskets. In reality, that species is a form of the native* Glechoma hederacea *or ground ivy, which could be considered for use as ground cover, although I avoid suggesting it because many people are allergic to its leaves. The real* Nepeta, *this one, is perhaps more familiarly known by its common name of catnip.* ❞

■ **CARE** Mulch lightly and apply a general fertilizer in spring. Cut back hard to soil level in late autumn.

■ **PROPAGATION** Lift and divide plants in spring. Sow seed of species in spring.

■ **PROBLEMS** Cats, which are irresistibly attracted to the plant and roll in and maul it. Handling the foliage can produce a skin rash in some people.

SIZE Varies, but within the range 30cm–1m x 30cm–1m (1–3ft x 1–3ft).
SITE AND SOIL Full sun and well-drained soil.
Weed Suppression Rating 3–4.
HARDINESS Varies, but forms recommended here are hardy to very hardy, tolerating about -20°C (-4°F).

■ **FEATURES** Herbaceous perennials with a loose, spreading habit. The flowers, which appear in summer in shades of white, blue and purple, are the main attraction. The foliage is grey-green and aromatic.

Recommended varieties
Nepeta cataria (catnip) the species most attractive to cats, aromatic grey-green foliage, white flowers, 75 x 30cm (30 x 12in) after 3 years, then 1m x 60cm (3 x 2 ft); *N. racemosa* (syn. *N. reichenbachiana*) spreading habit, aromatic grey-green foliage, deep violet or lilac-blue flowers, 30 x 60cm (12 x 24in), 'Snowflake' white flowers.

Nepeta racemosa

Omphalodes

❝ Omphalodes *was one of the first plants that I introduced into my garden, mainly because I had a rather prominent small bed at the front of the house that was, as gardeners say, 'tricky'. It was shaded and dry. I improved the moisture content but couldn't do anything about the shade. I planted* Omphalodes *because I liked it, and it spread wonderfully and is there still.* ❞

■ **CARE** Mulch and apply general fertilizer in spring. Cut away browned foliage in early spring.
■ **PROPAGATION** Divide plants in spring or in autumn. Sow seed in spring or take basal cuttings in early summer.
■ **PROBLEMS** None.

Omphalodes cappadocica

■ **FEATURES** Herbaceous, almost evergreen, perennials grown for their masses of blue flowers.

SIZE *O. cappadocica* 25 x 30–45cm (10 x 12–18in).
SITE AND SOIL Shady position and fairly moist, humus-rich soil.
Weed Suppression Rating 3.
HARDINESS Very hardy, tolerating -20°C (-4°F) or below, but may be browned by cold winds.

Recommended varieties
Omphalodes cappadocica AGM dense clumps from spreading rhizomes, glossy, oval green leaves, branching sprays of electric-blue flowers in spring with a few more in late summer, the best-coloured form.

Origanum Oregano, wild marjoram

" *Not many kitchen herbs are very successful as ground cover plants, largely because they tend to become untidy after a few years and need replacing. Oregano is perhaps best lifted and divided fairly frequently, but it is certainly more tidy than most – and in spring the golden-coloured form is utterly lovely.* "

■ **CARE** Apply a light dressing of general fertilizer in spring. Cut back hard to soil level in autumn.
■ **PROPAGATION** Take semi-ripe cuttings in summer or early autumn.
■ **PROBLEMS** May need renewing every three to four years.
■ **FEATURES** Aromatic, herbaceous perennials with small leaves in varying shades of green or gold. Small white or purple flowers appear in summer which are attractive to bees.

SIZE Varies within the range 20–45 x 20–30cm (8–18 x 8–12in).
SITE AND SOIL Full sun or light shade, golden forms do best in light shade. Tolerates most soils, but fertile and well-drained site preferred.
Weed Suppression Rating 2–3.
HARDINESS Varies, but form recommended here is very hardy, tolerating -20°C (-4°F).

Recommended varieties
Origanum vulgare 'Aureum' (golden wild marjoram) AGM golden-leaved form, leaves become greener in late summer, flowers insignificant, 30 x 30cm (12 x 12in).

Origanum vulgare '**Aureum**'

PERENNIALS AND ALPINES

Persicaria Knotweed

❝ *Mention knotweed and some people will immediately think of Japanese knotweed and feel that their interest in ground cover is waning rapidly. However, although close relatives, the plants I suggest here are in a different and altogether more civilized league. They are relatively both lower and slower growing.* ❞

Persicaria bistorta 'Superba'

■ **CARE** Little special care necessary, but general fertilizer may be applied in spring.
■ **PROPAGATION** Raise species from seed sown in spring, or lift and divide plants in autumn or spring.
■ **PRUNING** Remove faded flowerheads at the end of the season.
■ **PROBLEMS** May be invasive unless lifted and divided every two years.
■ **FEATURES** Easy-to-grow herbaceous perennials with long-lasting flowers in shades of pink, red or white. Some have autumn tints to the foliage.

SIZE Varies greatly (see Recommended varieties).
SITE AND SOIL Full sun or light shade and any moist but well-drained soil.
Weed Suppression Rating 3.
HARDINESS Very hardy, tolerating -20°C (-4°F).

Recommended varieties
Persicaria bistorta (syn. *Polygonum bistorta*; bistort), thick and fast-growing cover, light green leaves, club-like spikes of pale pink or white flowers in early summer, 75 x 60cm (30 x 24in), 'Superba' AGM clear pink flowers; *P. campanulata* (lesser knotweed) compact mat, ribbed mid-green leaves with pale brown undersides, branching clusters of pale pink flowers from late summer to early autumn, 1 x 1m (3 x 3ft); *P. vacciniifolia* AGM trailing mat, pointed leathery leaves with autumn tints, pink flower spikes in later summer to early autumn, 20 x 60cm (8 x 24in).

Petasites Butterbur

❝ *The wild butterbur,* Petasites hybridus, *was one of the aromas of my childhood, as it used to grow in profusion between the stream and the railway embankment where we stood to photograph passing steam trains. Although it certainly covered the ground, I'd be reluctant to suggest anything with quite such spicy pungency as a garden plant. These two relatives, however, while no great beauties, have much more charm and they certainly offer effective and robust ground cover in wilder spots.* ❞

■ **CARE** No special care necessary, but may be mulched and general fertilizer applied in spring. Dead-head as the flowers fade.
■ **PROPAGATION** Divide in autumn or spring.
■ **PROBLEMS** May be very invasive.
■ **FEATURES** Early-flowering perennials with small flowers in heads and large, almost rhubarb-like leaves.

SIZE *P. fragrans* 30cm x 1.2m (1 x 4ft), *P. japonicus giganteus* 1 x 2.5m (3 x 8ft).
SITE AND SOIL Shady, damp site preferred, good at the edge of a water garden.
Weed Suppression Rating 3.
HARDINESS Varies, *P. fragrans* is fairly hardy, tolerating about -5°C (23°F) but top growth may be killed in a bad winter, *P. japonicus* var. *giganteus* is hardy, tolerating -15 to -20°C (5 to -4°F).

Petasites fragrans

Recommended varieties

Petasites fragrans (fragrant butterbur, winter heliotrope) scented, small pale lilac flowers in late winter to early spring, followed by large rounded leaves, dark green with grey undersides; *P. japonicus* var. *giganteus* yellow-white flowers in late winter to early spring, very large and shiny light green leaves.

Phlox

❝ Phlox *is another of those 'big and small' genera – strapping big border perennials, little annual bedding plants and a handful of alpines, of which my recommendation here is one. It's another of those plants to avoid in a small alpine trough, but wonderful if you want to create an alpine meadow.* ❞

■ **CARE** No special care necessary, but benefits from general fertilizer in spring. Clip lightly after flowering to maintain tidiness.

■ **PROPAGATION** Take semi-ripe cuttings in summer (it is often possible to pull away a small rooted portion at the stem base).

■ **PROBLEMS** None for the low-growing perennial forms.

■ **FEATURES** Varied genus, but it does include low-growing perennial forms that may be used as ground cover. These have a cushion- or mat-like habit and produce a profusion of short-stemmed flowers in early spring to early summer.

SIZE 8 x 30cm (3 x 12in).
SITE AND SOIL Full sun and well-drained soil essential.
Weed Suppression Rating 2.
HARDINESS Vary hardy, tolerating -20°C (-4°F).

Recommended varieties

Phlox douglasii has numerous varieties, some more compact than the species, specific colours available include shades of pink, violet, red and white.

Phlox douglasii

Phuopsis

❝ There are two garden plants that can delude you into thinking that you have foxes in your garden. The crown imperial (Fritillaria imperialis) *is one of them, but you really have to disturb the bulbs to create the aroma. Phuopsis is the other, and this one needs no prompting. Many a time I have seen visitors standing close to a clump in my own garden wondering how close the fox must be. But smell aside, this is a pretty, rather delicate-looking but robust enough relative of the wild bedstraws. ❞*

■ **CARE** Little care necessary, but benefits from general fertilizer in spring. Best cut back after flowering to keep the plant tidy.

■ **PROPAGATION** Divide plants in spring or take semi-ripe cuttings in early summer. Sow seed of the species in autumn.

Phuopsis stylosa 'Purpurea'

■ **PROBLEMS** None.
■ **FEATURES** There is only one species, a low-growing, very aromatic hardy perennial with a carpet of summer flowers that attract butterflies. Plants usually die back in winter but will retain their leaves in mild areas.

SIZE 15 x 50cm (6 x 20in).
SITE AND SOIL Full sun or light shade. Well-drained soil essential.
Weed Suppression Rating 3.
HARDINESS Very hardy, tolerating -20°C (-4°F).

Recommended varieties
Phuopsis stylosa (syn. *Crucianella stylosa*) pale green leaves, pink tubular flowers, pungent aroma of foxes, 'Purpurea' deeper purple-pink flowers.

Prunella Self-heal

❝ Less familiar as a garden plant than a wild one, in the form of the native Prunella vulgaris, *this is nonetheless a genus of pretty, mat-forming plants, most at home when growing among turf. Be aware, however, that, like* Nepeta, *these plants can produce skin allergies in some people. ❞*

■ **CARE** Apply general fertilizer in spring, mulch well and water in dry spells over the summer. Dead-head to prevent self-seeding. Handle with care as some people develop skin rashes.
■ **PROPAGATION** Divide in spring or autumn. Sow seed of species in spring.

Prunella vulgaris

■ **PROBLEMS** Slugs, snails; may become very invasive.

■ **FEATURES** Creeping herbaceous or semi-evergreen perennials that form an easy-to-grow, weed-suppressing mat. The small flower spikes of pink, purple or white appear from midsummer onwards.

SIZE 30cm x 1m (1 x 3ft).
SITE AND SOIL Sun or partial shade. Tolerant of most soils, but best reserved for wilder parts of the garden.
Weed Suppression Rating 3.
HARDINESS Very hardy, tolerating -20°C (-4°F).

Recommended varieties
Prunella grandiflora (syn. *P. x webbiana*) deep green leaves, purple flowers in upright spikes, 'Loveliness', pink flowers, 'White Loveliness' white flowers; *P. laciniata* deeply cut leaves, cream flowers; *P. vulgaris* (syn. *P. incisa*) deeply cut leaves, deep purple flowers.

Pulmonaria Lungwort

❝ *Along with the yellow of primroses, the appearance of the bright blue flowers of* Pulmonaria *which accompany them is one of the most welcome signs of spring in my garden. But it was only after making a fairly large planting of pulmonarias and seeing the way they knitted together after a couple of seasons that I really began to appreciate their value as ground cover.* ❞

■ **CARE** Ensure the planting position is well prepared with organic matter, as the plants are intolerant of dryness. Apply general fertilizer in spring and

SIZE 15-25 x 30–45cm (6-10 x 12–18in).
SITE AND SOIL Moist soil in partial shade gives best results. Grow in full sun only if soil is kept moist in summer, although *P. angustifolia* prefers an open position and fairly light soil.
Weed Suppression Rating 3.
HARDINESS Very hardy, tolerating -20°C (-4°F).

Recommended varieties
Pulmonaria angustifolia AGM earliest to bloom with bright blue flowers, plain green leaves, 'Munstead Blue' deep blue flowers; *P. officinalis* heart-shaped leaves blotched with pale green or white, deep pink buds open to clusters of flowers that change colour from pink to violet-blue, 'Sissinghurst White' AGM vigorous, pale pink buds, white flowers; *P. rubra* (syn. *P. angustifolia* 'Rubra', *P. officinalis* subsp. *rubra*) AGM vigorous, large plain green leaves, early pink-red flowers, 45 x 1m (18in x 3ft), 'Barfield Pink' less vigorous, white and pink striped flowers; *P. saccharata* Argentea Group AGM evergreen foliage heavily spotted with silver, pink flowers.

trim back untidy or browned foliage.
■ **PROPAGATION** Division in autumn is the best method, but seed of the species may be sown outdoors in spring.
■ **PROBLEMS** Powdery mildew.
■ **FEATURES** Pretty, early-flowering perennials for shady areas. They are easy to grow and most have attractive foliage for much of the year.

Pulmonaria 'Munstead Blue'

PERENNIALS AND ALPINES

Saxifraga

❝ *Forget about those little clump-forming alpines that you have in your trough or rock garden and think about one of the larger, more robust members of this very big genus (more than 300 species). London pride is certainly an old variety, one of those plants that parents and grandparents remember having in their gardens, but as far as I'm concerned time hasn't dimmed either its features or its value.* ❞

■ **CARE** No special care necessary, but benefits from general fertilizer or bonemeal in spring. Cut off flower stems in early summer when flowering is over.

■ **PROPAGATION** Detach rosettes and root them as cuttings in late spring to early summer.

■ **PROBLEMS** None.

■ **FEATURES** Large genus of cushion- or rosette-forming rock plants, but

SIZE 10 x 60cm (4 x 24in) after 3 years, 25–30cm (10–12in) tall when in flower. Spread indefinite but easily controlled.
SITE AND SOIL Tolerates most positions and soils, but ideal for light shade.
Weed Suppression Rating 2–3.
HARDINESS Very hardy, tolerating -20°C (-4°F) or below.

Saxifraga x urbium

S. x *urbium* is an easy and more vigorous form that makes attractive ground cover. It offers year-round, fresh green foliage in the form of leaf rosettes. In early summer there are airy clusters of pale pink or white flowers.

Recommended varieties
Saxifraga x *urbium* (syn. *S. umbrosa*; London pride) AGM fresh green leaf rosettes, small star-shaped flowers smother the plants in late spring.

Sedum

❝ *Like* Saxifraga, Sedum *is another rock garden genus, and similarly it is one that has some larger, more robust members. But some of them also have a rather special propensity for multiplying, small pieces breaking off very readily to root nearby, rather in the manner of self-sown seedlings. Do be aware of this whenever you introduce these ground cover forms into your garden.* ❞

■ **CARE** No special care necessary, but benefits from general fertilizer or bonemeal in spring.

■ **PROPAGATION** Divide or take cuttings of non-flowering shoots in spring. Sow seed of species in spring.

■ **PROBLEMS** Aphids, mealy bugs, vine weevil.

■ **FEATURES** Succulents of various sizes and shapes, ideal for covering dry sites. Their main feature is the colour and texture of the foliage, but many have star-like flowers from summer to autumn.

Recommended varieties

Sedum acre (biting stonecrop) creeping evergreen mat, which fragments easily to produce stem 'cuttings' that spread widely, pale green foliage, yellow flowers in early summer, 5 x 15cm (2 x 6in); *S. album* sprawling habit, cigar-shaped, shiny leaves, white flowers in midsummer, evergreen but best cut back hard each autumn, 15 x 30cm (6 x 12in), thereafter spreads 30cm (12in) a year; *S. anacampseros* creeping tuber with lax stems, long, fleshy, blue-green foliage, semi-evergreen, purple flowers in mid- to late summer, 10cm x 1m (4in x 3ft) to indefinite; *S. cauticola* AGM herbaceous, unkempt habit with creeping stems, fleshy blue-green foliage with purple tints, purple flowers in autumn, 10 x 30cm (4 x 12in); *S. kamtschaticum* var. *floriferum* 'Weihenstephaner Gold' semi-evergreen, lax fleshy stems, mid-green leaves, plentiful flowering shoots with deep yellow flowers from summer until mid-autumn, 10 x 60cm (4 x 24in); *S. rupestre* (syn. *S. forsterianum*, *S. reflexum*) evergreen mat, fleshy blue-green foliage, yellow flowers in midsummer, 20 x 60cm (8 x 24in); *S. sexangulare* slender creeping stems, evergreen mat with green leaves, yellow flowers in summer, 8 x 60cm (3 x 24in).

SIZE Height 5–20cm (2–8in), spread 15cm (6in) to indefinite.
SITE AND SOIL Sunny site preferred, but *S. cauticola* enjoys light shade. Any soil except cold and wet. Tolerant of dry sites.
Weed Suppression Rating 2.
HARDINESS Very hardy, tolerating -20°C (-4°F) or below.

Sedum rupestre

Stachys Lamb's ears, Lamb's tongue

❝ *The ground cover* Stachys *is a plant that children love. They stroke its soft woolly leaves just as they would a pet rabbit, or indeed a pet lamb, hence the common names. It is certainly an unusual, distinctive ground cover species and its only real drawback is that those soft woolly 'ears' do sometimes become unattractively spotted.* ❞

■ **CARE** Apply general fertilizer in spring and cut off the flowerheads to maintain a silver carpet effect.
■ **PROPAGATION** Divide in spring or sow seed sown in spring.
■ **PROBLEMS** Leaf spots, rots.
■ **FEATURES** Herbaceous perennial producing silver-grey carpets of foliage. There are flowers but these are best removed, or choose non-flowering forms.

SIZE 40 x 50cm (16 x 20in).
SITE AND SOIL Full sun and any well-drained soil. Good choice for dry or coastal gardens.
Weed Suppression Rating 3–4.
HARDINESS Very hardy, tolerating -20°C (-4°F).

Recommended varieties

Stachys byzantina (syn. *S. lanata*; lamb's ears) dense mat of woolly grey foliage, tiny mauve-pink flowers on leafy spikes in summer, 'Silver Carpet', silver foliage and no flowers.

Stachys byzantina 'Silver Carpet'

Symphytum Comfrey

❝ *By no stretch of anyone's imagination is comfrey an attractive garden plant; in truth, it comes as close to being 'functional' as any that I know. Most gardeners indeed grow it for no better purpose that to make compost from it. There are, however, a few rather more appealing varieties, and if you want rather coarse, rather functional ground cover for an area of the garden where aesthetics don't matter too much, this will achieve it.* ❞

■ **CARE** No special care necessary, but mulch while it is establishing if the soil is dry and apply general fertilizer in spring. Remove faded flowers and foliage.

■ **PROPAGATION** Divide in autumn or spring.

■ **PROBLEMS** None.

■ **FEATURES** Comfrey is well known to organic gardeners for its use as a soil improver or ingredient of the compost heap, but there are some more ornamental forms that are ideal ground cover for shady sites. They are grown for their oval or lance-shaped leaves and spikes of late-spring flowers.

SIZE 30–60 x 45–60cm (12–24 x 18–24in), named varieties smaller than species.
SITE AND SOIL Any shaded position, ideally moist although tolerant of most soils.
Weed Suppression Rating 4.
HARDINESS Very hardy, tolerating at least -20°C (-4°F)

Recommended varieties
Symphytum caucasicum hairy mid-green leaves, red-purple or blue flowers in early summer; 'Goldsmith' bright green foliage edged with cream and gold, white, blue or pink flowers in early spring; 'Hidcote Blue' mauve-blue and white flowers in late spring to early summer.

Symphytum caucasicum 'Hidcote Blue'

Tanacetum

❝ *Rather after the manner of its close relative yarrow (*Achillea*, see p. 58), tansy (*Tanacetum vulgare*) is a unsophisticated plant, often found in its native weedy state but nonetheless with some more ornamental garden forms, too. It is strongly but not unpleasantly aromatic and is useful for covering the soil in wilder parts of the garden.* ❞

■ **CARE** Apply general fertilizer in spring and dead-head faded blooms regularly to promote further flowering.

■ **PROPAGATION** Divide in spring. Sow seed of species in spring.

■ **PROBLEMS** None, but *T. vulgare* can spread a considerable distance through self-seeding.

■ **FEATURES** Hardy perennials with daisy or button-like summer flowers. Many also have decorative and aromatic foliage.

SIZE Varies greatly (see Recommended varieties).
SITE AND SOIL Open, sunny position and well-drained soil.
Weed Suppression Rating 3.
HARDINESS Varies, but forms recommended here are very hardy, tolerating -20°C (-4°F).

Recommended varieties
Tanacetum argenteum (syn. *Achillea argentea*) evergreen mat, finely divided silver-grey foliage, small white daisies with yellow centres, 20 x 30cm (8 x 12in); *T. vulgare* (syn. *Chrysanthemum vulgare*; tansy) finely divided, bright green aromatic foliage, tiny button-like yellow flowers, 1m x 60cm (3 x 2ft), *T. v.* var. *crispum* (crisp-leaved tansy), crisp fern-like leaves, only 60cm (24in) tall.

Tellima

" I have referred to the more robust varieties of Saxifraga as unexpected ground cover. This plant isn't a saxifrage, but it is a member of the same family and, like its relative Heuchera, is a genus to which I have slowly become more attached. I have now almost reached the point where I think they are rather attractive. "

■ **CARE** Mulch if the foliage dies down fully. Apply general fertilizer in spring and dead-head after flowering.
■ **PROPAGATION** Divide in autumn or spring, or sow fresh seed in spring.
■ **PROBLEMS** None.
■ **FEATURES** Only one species, a herbaceous perennial with a tendency to be evergreen in mild areas. A woodland plant, rather like *Heuchera*, it produces a clump of leaves with flower spikes that appear above the foliage in late spring to early summer.

Tellima grandiflora

SIZE 45 x 45cm (18 x 18in), up to 60–75cm (24–30in) tall when in flower.
SITE AND SOIL Prefers light shade but can cope with sun or deeper shade. Cool, moist but well-drained soil preferred, but worth trying on most soils.
Weed Suppression Rating 2–3.
HARDINESS Hardy, tolerating about -15°C (-5°F).

Recommended varieties
Tellima grandiflora light green hairy leaves, upright stems with small green-yellow flowers that age to pink.

Thalictrum

" For gardeners everywhere, Thalictrum is the meadow rue, a lovely tall perennial for damp places and a native plant with some striking exotic relatives. But you need look no further than the hedgerows or wild grassy places to find this dwarf species, which will fool many people into thinking you have a massed planting of maidenhair fern. "

■ **CARE** Mulch and apply general fertilizer in spring. Cut back flowered stems after flowering.
■ **PROPAGATION** Divide in spring, replant naturally rooted runners, or sow fresh seed in late summer or autumn.
■ **PROBLEMS** Invasive in a rich, fertile soil.

■ **FEATURES** Most *Thalictrum* species are medium to tall border plants with masses of summer blooms, but *T. minus* is a ground cover species that looks rather like a maidenhair fern.

SIZE 30 x 20cm (12 x 8in), but more or less indefinite spread by runners.
SITE AND SOIL Light to deep shade preferred. Best in moist, humus-rich, alkaline soil, but tolerates most sites.
Weed Suppression Rating 3.
HARDINESS Very hardy, tolerating -20°C (-4°F) or below.

Recommended varieties
Thalictrum minus pale green leaves, each up to 25cm (10in) long and made up of deeply lobed leaflets, fluffy clusters of small creamy yellow flowers.

Thalictrum minus

Thymus Thyme

❝ *No herb garden is complete without its complement of thymes, although for culinary purposes you should be growing some of the tufted, clump-forming varieties, which have the best flavour. But nor is any consideration of ground cover complete without thymes, because the low-growing, mat-forming culti-vated forms or, even better, some of the species, will produce a carpet that is both attractive and durable enough to be walked on.* ❞

■ **CARE** Mulch lightly and apply a little general fertilizer in spring.
■ **PROPAGATION** Take semi-ripe cuttings in late summer. Sow seed of species in either spring or autumn.

■ **PROBLEMS** None, but worth replacing plants with cuttings every three years or so.
■ **FEATURES** Creeping or bushy evergreen perennials, with small but attractive, aromatic leaves in shades of green, silver or gold. Small pink, white or purple flowers appear in summer.

SIZE Prostrate forms around 5 x 25–30cm (2 x 10–12in).
SITE AND SOIL Full sun and well-drained soil. Particularly successful in alkaline gardens. On heavy soils, dig in organic matter or grit when planting.
Weed Suppression Rating 3–4.
HARDINESS Hardy, tolerating -15 to -20°C (5 to -4°F).

Thymus 'Doone Valley'

Recommended varieties
Thymus caespititius prostrate spreader, bright green leaves, purple to pale pink flowers; 'Doone Valley' shrubby habit, dark green leaves with yellow markings, purple-pink flowers, 10 x 20cm (4 x 8in); 'Porlock' prostrate mat, glossy dark green leaves, purple or white flowers; *T. serpyllum* (creeping thyme, wild thyme) prostrate mat, dark green leaves, purple or white flowers, 'Annie Hall' shell-pink flowers, 'Pink Chintz' grey-green leaves, small pink flowers.

Tiarella Foam flower

❝ *Tiarella is one of the first plants you will see if you visit my garden. It covers a small bed in a rather awkward spot – slightly shaded, slightly dry and an area that I am fairly content to leave to its own devices. Plant it, as I do, along with* Heuchera, Tellima *and* Omphalodes *for a very agreeable effect. After a few years you will appreciate the common name as the flowers float like foam over the foliage.* ❞

■ **CARE** Mulch and apply general fertil-izer in spring.
■ **PROPAGATION** Divide in spring or autumn.
■ **PROBLEMS** None.
■ **FEATURES** Evergreen perennials valued for their fresh green foliage and sprays of creamy white flowers in early summer.

Tiarella wherryi

SIZE 15–25 x 25–45cm (6–10 x 10–18in), although *T. cordifolia* is 23cm x 1m (9in x 3ft).
SITE AND SOIL Cool, shady position preferred and tolerates moderately dry soils.
Weed Suppression Rating 3.
HARDINESS Very hardy, tolerating -20°C (-4°F) or below.

Recommended varieties
Tiarella cordifolia AGM mat spreads rapidly, pale green leaves with bronze tints in winter, white blooms; *T. polyphylla* clump forming, rhizomatous roots, mid-green leaves, creamy white flowers; *T. wherryi* (syn. *T. collina*) AGM compact clump, leaves turn russet-brown in autumn, pink or white flowers.

Trifolium Clover

" *If you have a lawn, the chances are that you won't need me to tell you that clover is good ground cover. If you aren't careful, it will be so good that it will take over from your grass – and it tends to be rather tolerant of most lawn weedkillers. But by all means, turn this to your advantage if you want a green, non-grass growth in another part of your garden.* "

■ **CARE** Apply general fertilizer in spring.
■ **PROPAGATION** Divide in spring or sow seed of the species in autumn; self-seeds readily.
■ **PRUNING** Dead-head if untidy.
■ **FEATURES** Clover makes good ground cover but some species may become invasive. The main attraction is the tiny flowers in summer, which are loved by bees. Each leaf is composed of from four to seven leaflets.

SIZE 15–30 x 60cm (6–12 x 24in).
SITE AND SOIL Open, sunny position required. Thrives in most soils.
Weed Suppression Rating 4.
HARDINESS Very hardy, tolerating -20°C (-4°F) or below.

Recommended varieties
Trifolium pratense (purple clover) semi-evergreen, bushy, dark green leaves, red-purple to pink flowers in midsummer, 'Susan Smith' dark pink flowers, leaves have gold veins; *T. repens* (white clover, shamrock) best known as a lawn weed, semi-evergreen, creeping stems, dark green leaves, scented white flowers from late spring to early autumn, 'Purpurascens' red-brown leaflets edged with green, 'Purpurascens Quadrifolium' is similar but with four or more leaflets.

Trifolium pratense 'Susan Smith'

PERENNIALS AND ALPINES

Verbena

❝ Verbena *is one of the main-stays of container planting in summer, where the half-hardy varieties of* V. x hybrida *in their reds, purples, pinks and white blend well with fuchsias and other popular container plants. But there are hardy species, too, and the South American* V. corymbosa *is a rather attractive plant that I have found particularly good at spreading across warm, sunny beds.* ❞

■ **CARE** Apply general fertilizer in spring.
■ **PROPAGATION** Divide in spring or take softwood cuttings in spring.
■ **PROBLEMS** Aphids, tarsonemid mites, powdery mildew.

■ **FEATURES** Genus containing both hardy perennials (recommended here) and half-hardy bedding plants with flowers in shades of blue, pink, red, purple and white. The habit varies greatly, but dense terminal clusters of small flowers are the main feature.

SIZE *V. corymbosa* 1.2 x 1m (4 x 3ft).
SITE AND SOIL Warm, sunny spot and fertile, moist soil.
Weed Suppression Rating 2–3.
HARDINESS Fairly hardy, tolerating about -5 to -10°C (23 to 14°F).

Recommended varieties
Verbena corymbosa underground rhizomes, triangular mid-green leaves, small lilac flowers, may be invasive in damp sites.

Veronica

❝ *Veronicas are popularly called speedwells and one of their number,* Veronica filiformis, *is responsible for the 'blue lawns' that you either love or hate. It is a very common and difficult-to-control lawn weed that, rather like clover, doesn't respond well to most weedkillers. There are other spreading veronicas, too, all characterized by the same small, electric-blue flowers. They are unlikely to become lawn weeds but will produce a similar blue carpet where you do plant them.* ❞

■ **CARE** Mulch and apply general fertilizer in spring. Lift and divide every two to three years to keep plants growing strongly. Dead-head regularly.

Verbena corymbosa

Veronica prostrata 'Mrs Holt'

■ **PROPAGATION** Divide in autumn or spring. Sow seed of species in early spring.

■ **PROBLEMS** Powdery mildew.

■ **FEATURES** Hardy perennials, some evergreen, grown for their blue flowers in summer.

SIZE Varies greatly (see Recommended varieties).

SITE AND SOIL Sunny site, sheltered from cold winds. Tolerant of most soils but best in light, alkaline conditions.

Weed Suppression Rating 2–3.

HARDINESS Hardy, tolerating -15 to -20°C (5 to -4°F).

Recommended varieties

Veronica austriaca evergreen, upright but floppy habit, downy oval leaves, clear blue flowers from early to midsummer, needs winter cover in cold, wet areas, 20 x 60cm (8 x 24in); *V. beccabunga* (brooklime) floppy habit, dark green leaves, starry blue flowers with violet veins in late spring to early summer, needs moist soil, often grown as a pond marginal, 60 x 60cm (24 x 24in); *V. nummularia* (Pyrenean speedwell) evergreen, mat-like rock plant, fleshy leaves, clusters of blue or pink flowers, 5 x 30cm (2 x 12in); *V. prostrata* (syn. *V. rupestris*) AGM evergreen, mat-like rock plant, bright blue flowers from late spring to early summer, 10 x 45cm (4 x 18in), 'Blue Sheen' bright blue flowers, 'Mrs Holt' pink flowers, 'Trehane' violet-blue flowers, yellow-green foliage.

Viola

❝ *The genus* Viola, *including as it does violets, violas and pansies, has long been a much-loved member of our garden flora. In recent years, the development of new and very hardy varieties of winter-flowering pansy has popularized the group even more. But in taking advantage of the bedding pansy, in both winter and summer, don't forget the ground-covering value of the perennial, carpeting species for wilder parts of your garden.* ❞

■ **CARE** Apply a light dressing of general fertilizer in spring. Dead-head to promote further flowering.

■ **PROPAGATION** Take basal cuttings in midsummer or sow seed in spring.

■ **PROBLEMS** Mosaic virus, rust.

■ **FEATURES** Most are hardy, evergreen perennials but are often treated as short-lived plants. They are grown for their cheerful flowers, which are flat with five petals in a wide range of colours.

SIZE 5–10 x 30cm (2–4 x 12in).

SITE AND SOIL Sun or partial shade. Tolerant of most soils, but may fail on sites where related species of *Viola* have been grown repeatedly.

Weed Suppression Rating 3.

HARDINESS Very hardy, tolerating -20°C (-4°F).

Recommended varieties

Viola alba (syn. *V. obliqua* subsp. *alba*) white flowers with violet veins in late spring to early summer, best in some shade; *V. biflora* (yellow wood violet) bright yellow flowers in spring, best in some shade; *V. riviniana* (dog violet) blue-violet flowers with spurs, flowers from early spring to early autumn, may be invasive – notorious for invading lawns.

Viola riviniana

INDEX

Page numbers in *italics* refer to illustrations.

94

PHOTOGRAPHIC ACKNOWLEDGEMENTS

A–Z Botanical Collection 26, 78, 92 left/Andrew Alderley 60/Bob Gibbons 58 right/Julia Hancock 36/Malcolm Richards 69/Dan Sams 11/John Stiles 17/Adrian Thomas Photography 87 right
Garden Matters 33 right
Garden Picture Library/Mark Bolton 82/Philippe Bonduel 14 bottom/Brian Carter 25 bottom, 35, 45 right/Eric Crichton 9 top, 52/Ron Evans 54 right/Christopher Fairweather 14 top left/John Glover 20, 37 right, 38 right, 53 left, 53 right, 83 right, 86, 92 right/Sunniva Harte 37 left, 90/Neil Holmes 19, 34 right, 39, 47 left, 47 right, 79 left/Lamontagne 51, 88/Jerry Pavia 30 left/Laslo Puskas 41 right/Howard Rice 5 bottom, 7, 28, 44, 45 left, 81 left, 91 left/J.S. Sira 14 top right, 76/Didier Willery 12, 57, 84
John Glover 74 left

Harpur Garden Library 4, 25 top, 30 right, 33 left, 46, 65, 85 bottom, back cover/Beth Chatto 8, 9 bottom/Kelvinside, Natal 6 bottom
Andrew Lawson front cover, 2–3, 5 top, 6 top, 13 bottom, 21, 27 bottom, 32, 43 right, 61 left, 71 left, 72, 73 top, 73 bottom, 74 right, 75, 81 right, 83 left, 89 left, 91 right, 93
Octopus Publishing Group Ltd 1 top, 1 bottom, 2, 13 top, 16, 23, 24, 31, 40, 41 left, 42, 43 left, 49 left, 55, 56, 58 left, 59, 61 right, 62, 64, 66 right, 67, 68, 70, 71 right, 77, 79 right, 80
Photos Horticultural 10, 22, 34 left, 54 left, 87 left
Harry Smith Collection 18, 27 top, 29, 38 left, 48, 49 right, 50, 63, 66 left, 85 top, 89 right